The Children's Media Yearbook is a publication of The Children's Media Foundation

Director, Greg Childs
Administrator, Jacqui Wells

The Children's Media Foundation
15 Briarbank Rd
London
W13 0HH

info@thechildrensmediafoundation.org

First published 2019

ISBN 978-1-9161353-0-7

Book design by Camilla Umar

The Children's Media
FOUNDATION

ALCS

DO YOU WRITE SCRIPTS, BOOKS OR ARTICLES?

- ALCS is a membership organisation run by writers, for writers

- Since 1977 we have paid over £500m to writers

- Join 100,000 other writers in the UK and across the world and become a Member

Find out more and join online >> **alcs.co.uk**

AUTHORS' LICENSING AND COLLECTING SOCIETY
PROTECTING AND PROMOTING AUTHORS' RIGHTS

CBeebies
BBC

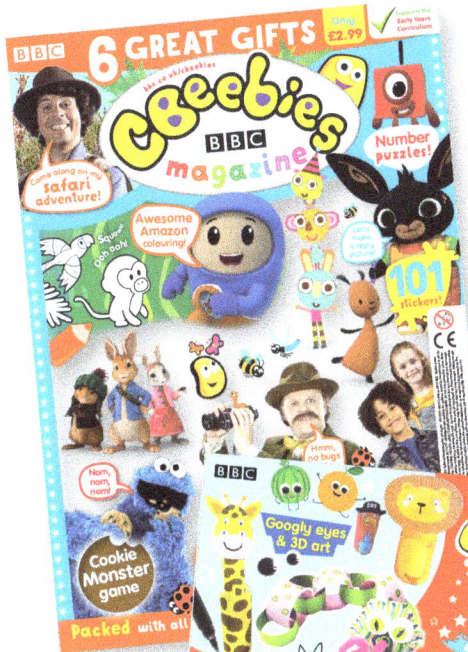

- **CBeebies** is the biggest brand in pre-school magazines, with **19.2%** of the pre-school market!*

- **CBeebies Magazine** is the UK's best-selling children's compilation magazine.

- The **CBeebies** portfolio sells over **200,000** copies a month.

- The CBeebies portfolio is up **4%** year on year. *

- CBeebies Special had the biggest year on year increase in pre-school, it's up **14%**!*

- CBeebies Magazine is up **5%** year on year.*

*UK wholesale data Jan – Apr 2019

**ABCs Jan – Dec 2018

Clangers
50th

2019 celebrates 50 years
of love, kindness and whistles!

clangers.com

© 2019 Coolabi Productions Limited, Smallfilms Limited and Peter Firmin.

coolabi

THE
CHILDREN'S
MEDIA
CONFERENCE
2,3 & 4 JULY 2019
SHEFFIELD UK

The Children's Media Conference is proud
to support the Children's Media Foundation
in its pursuit of the best possible media
choices for children and young people
in the UK.
www.thechildrensmediaconference.com

jam

is a proud supporter of
the Children's Media Foundatio

CHILDREN'S MEDIA YEARBOOK 2019

Sixteen South

CREATING STORIES FOR EVERY CHILD IN EVERY HOME IN EVERY COUNTRY

Those Licensing People Ltd.™

is a proud supporter of
the Children's Media Foundation

EDITOR'S RABBIT

MARK WILSON

Photo by TaiLi Samson on Unsplash

Hey! Dear Reader!

Don't skip this bit. Meaty stuff to follow – news, policy, learning, research, production, consumption – but first indulge me for a mo.

Step back in time: it's three weeks before the Yearbook goes to the printer; I'm bleary-eyed, show tunes on shuffle, gawping at the Contents List. Gobsmacked.

What a stunning selection of articles from a diverse range of authors, photographers and illustrators, who've all contributed for no fee, without so much as a grumble (despite me nagging when deadlines loom).

I can't say it loud enough, or in a big enough font: **HUMONGOUS THANKS** to all you wonderful content providers (Becky, Camilla and Tom, too!) for making the CMF's 2019 Yearbook such an insightful and entertaining read; a permanent record of children's media during these turbulent but cautiously optimistic times.

Now, a reminder before you forge ahead: please show your coffee-stained, dog-eared Yearbook to friends and colleagues. Better still – twist their arms to buy a fresh copy! They can be downloaded, or glossy, wipe-clean paperbacks purchased, via: www. thechildrensmediafoundation.org/childrens-media-yearbook-2019

If you join us as a *supporter* or *patron*, or attach your company as a *corporate supporter*, you'll be helping the CMF to help the UK's children's media industry be the best it can be. Our only source of funding is donations, so if you're as passionate as we are about the children's audience, please become one of our supporters: www. thechildrensmediafoundation.org/support

Finally, this is where I'm supposed to summarise the rest of the book. And yet, with so many thought-provoking, illuminating, poignant and controversial articles, a précis wouldn't do them justice. However I *can* say (no spoilers!) that the Children's Media Yearbook 2019 definitely contains the following words:

CATERPILLAR ... ACTIVIST ... CLOWN ... BIKINI ... FUND ... TOMBOLA ... PICASSO... NINJA ... E-TAIL ... BREXIT ... GOD ... GIANTS EGGBOTS ... WILL YOUNG ... and "GRRR!"

Oh, and a few show tunes along the way – song titles as section headers. Guess the musical; answers near the end of the book. (Might come in handy if you're stuck at karaoke)

WELCOME FROM THE CHILDREN'S MEDIA FOUNDATION

GREG CHILDS

Director, The Children's Media Foundation

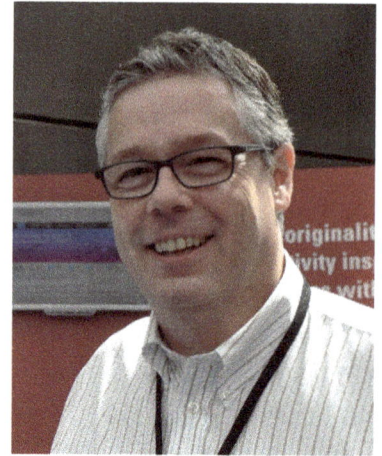

It's been a long time coming, but 2019 has seen real progress on many Children's Media Foundation campaign issues. Media-watchers and the children's television industry have expressed cautious optimism at measures which are being taken to alleviate chronic under-funding of children's content in the UK – to ensure a healthier, more plural, competitive approach to public service provision, and to improve the unsafe, uncaring environment children and young people experience through social media.

There's always more to be done, as CMF Chair Anna Home outlines in her article for this Yearbook on the policy landscape in 2019. But, without resting on our laurels, the Foundation can honestly claim that ideas we generated over ten years ago, and the lobbying which we have pursued since, have culminated in a series of initiatives which give the content industry hope – and which should provide the young people's audience in the UK with greater choice and more relevance, as well as potentially more appropriate methods of accessing content.

CMF launched in 2011 through the merger of the short-lived campaign Save Kids TV and the Children's Film and Television Foundation, which can trace its roots back to 1951. It was first set up as the Children's Film Foundation by Lord Rank, who lobbied for a levy on cinema tickets to subsidise British film production; the Eady Levy, as it became known, was in part used to fund the CFF to make features entirely dedicated to – and populated by – children. Over 175 films were made, which are now archived at the BFI (with some available on DVD).

That our origins were funded by a levy is an irony which is not lost on us at CMF. When we sprang into life in 2011, we launched a bold plan for a video-on-demand public service publisher, funded to commission content across the age ranges and designed to repair the "market failure"

Supporters pack out a CMF public meeting to discuss the YAC Fund, Ofcom and the PSBs. CMF fulfilling its remit of improving the public discourse around children's media

which the regulator Ofcom had identified as a defining feature of kids' media in the UK.

It gained little support at the time. But constant conversations with politicians and policy-makers, and quiet collaboration with industry bodies better equipped to campaign on the industry's behalf, have finally brought about significant change.

At first it was difficult to persuade political figures that "market failure" in children's media was anything more than an industry suffering a downturn. The cultural and societal implications had to be explained. Soon it became apparent that politicians of all parties were adopting our language in their statements about the need to take action.

Eight years on sees the launch of the Young Audiences Content Fund: a new

method of supporting content for the commercial public service broadcasters, empowering producers to pitch a wide range of innovative ideas which could

otherwise not achieve financing or reach their audience. The Fund is already in operation, dispersing £57 million of public finance over the next three years in an ambitious pilot. It's all intended entirely for children and young people – once again, the subject of last-minute lobbying to ensure the focus was not diluted.

Ofcom and the PSBs

At the same time, successful amendments to the Digital Economy Act have created a new regulatory power for Ofcom, to address the market failure if it sees the need. Ofcom's softly-softly approach is sensible given the restrictions on public service regulation and the way in which children and teenagers now watch content. Looking for a holistic approach by the three public service broadcasters, Ofcom wrote to them requiring that they outline their strategies to "do more".

This has encouraged each broadcaster to consider which audience segments it should address, what sort of content is needed (in a commercial environment) and which platforms are most appropriate to reach those audiences … as well as the ultimate question: how much they can afford to pay, when previously those budgets were extremely small. This is, of course, where the Young Audiences Content Fund enters the equation.

Online harms

So as the government uses rare "joined-up thinking" to enable UK broadcasters to compete with foreign competition from the big new providers, it's ironic to see the social media platforms that so dominate the lives of kids also coming under scrutiny. Once again, CMF led the conversation on the responsibilities of the operators of YouTube, Facebook, etc., to safeguard children and young people.

When we tackled them on how they could take greater care to avoid the multiple harms which it's now apparent the young are experiencing online, these platforms were dismissive. Their simple response (using the USA COPPA regulations as their shield) was that under 13s did not, or should not, be using their services. This, despite growing parental concern about just how those services *were* being used by the young; about just what they were viewing, sharing, experiencing and suffering there, and the effect this might have on their minds and lives.

Now, as the press and politicians jump eagerly into the fray – and social media platforms come under scrutiny for all sorts of ills, from vote-rigging to addictive behaviour – the issue of how children fare

Home Secretary Sajid Javid launching the government's Online Harms

online has come to the fore. The government has published what it claims will be a ground-breaking attempt to regulate the internet, if the platforms don't put their own houses in order. Facebook founders talk about breaking the company up; even Mark Zuckerberg advocates a form of quasi-voluntary regulation.

It remains to be seen whether the proposed legislation on "Online Harms" will have a meaningful effect, but that and other initiatives, such as new data-protection laws and the inclusion of a digital bill of rights in the UN Declaration of the Rights of the Child, along with commercial and customer pressure, are all indications that change must come.

The Children's Media Foundation was there raising these issues years ago – and we will continue to be there to ensure that change benefits UK kids.

Support and donations

To continue this work, we really need your help. The CMF survives entirely on the tireless voluntary work of its Board and Executive team, and the support of invaluable groups like our Academic Advisory Board. The existence of this Yearbook, for example, is a tribute to the volunteer efforts of its new editors Mark Wilson and Tom Cousins, to whom CMF is hugely indebted.

If you can offer your expertise and time, please do. If not, please follow the example of oth¢›ers in the children's media industry and donate. Become a supporter or patron, or sign up your company in support.

Your donations all go towards helping us look to the future of media for children and young people in the UK, and set the agenda for policy and regulatory discussions in the years ahead. ◉

Become a supporter or a patron:
www.thechildrensmediafoundation.org

THE CHILDREN'S MEDIA POLICY LANDSCAPE 2019

ANNA HOME OBE

Chair, the Children's Media Foundation

—

When I looked back at last year's Children's Media Yearbook, the opening line of my article considering the state of children's media in the UK was: "It has been a year of consultation, meetings and debate, and, as I write this in June, of very few definitive outcomes – yet."

Things have certainly progressed – and, as Greg Childs says in his introductory article, we have a lot to celebrate as we launch this Yearbook in time for the start of the Children's Media Conference 2019.

Aimed at both development and production, the Young Audiences Content Fund (YACF) is in place and is actively considering submissions with a great team at the BFI, led by Jackie Edwards. In the light of Ofcom's new requirements for more content for young people, the commercial PSBs are rethinking their policies regarding original content. And, after years of parental concern, the social media platforms are under greater scrutiny and the threat of regulation.

However, this neither means that all the problems are solved, nor that the Children's Media Foundation's job is done.

CMF will be following the progress of the YACF, considering the outcomes, how well they fulfil the original concept and how the criteria for selection work. We are pleased that we are represented on both the Strategic Advisory Group and the Steering Group of the fund, and so are well positioned to comment on its progress. Looking at the opportunities the Fund offers, we are confident that innovative and exciting projects will emerge.

But we must remember that this is just a three-year pilot. The government money supporting the Fund is a defined sum: £57 million. Until the outcomes have been assessed, no decisions will be made about continuing the Fund or where the finance might come from. If the Fund is to have a future – and, given the amount of time and effort which has been spent on it, it must – new sources of funding will have to be found, and put in place in time so that funding can continue seamlessly.

To be truly useful to the children's media industry, and truly serve the children's and youth audience, this funding has to be additional; not taken, wholly or partially, from the Television Licence Fee. CMF will certainly be pressing for this work to begin as soon as possible, and for new sources of finance for the Fund to be considered.

ITV

Equally, we will carefully monitor the progress of the new proposals from the commercial PSBs. The companies have not yet published the details of their responses to Ofcom's request that they increase output for kids and teens. It seems that all parties are intending to release their plans in time for CMC.

ITV has announced a budget increase for children's content, of approximately 10% – more than any other part of the organisation. It's from a low base point, of course; spending was heavily cut back in the last ten years, in the face of severely declining advertising revenues around children's content. This is a response to the Fund and is, once more, a cause for optimism. At time of writing they have also supported their first project through to application... Let's hope many more follow.

Channel 4

For several years, CMF has been particularly concerned about the failure of Channel 4 to fulfil its Broadcasting Licence requirement to provide content for older children and younger teens: the ten to fourteen year old audience. We do not believe that family programmes which may appeal to a younger audience (such as *Ackerly Bridge*) solve this problem.

We welcome the younger audience being considered when these programmes are put together, but that is not the same as making dedicated programmes aimed squarely at what concerns the young teenage audience – and inhabited by people like themselves. They have as much right as any segment of the audience to "hear their own voices and experience their own stories".

So we were delighted to learn from Channel 4, at the May 2019 CMF event "The Fund, Ofcom and the PSBs", that they are about to unveil a completely new strategy for the ten to fourteen year old audience. This is good news and we look forward to hearing the details. As you read this, those plans may well have been announced – just before the CMC, or at the conference's opening Question Time session, sponsored and produced by CMC and chaired by Stuart Purvis CBE.

BBC

The BBC has not been involved in these discussions, other than to express concerns that future iterations of the YACF might raid Licence Fee money. As a public service broadcaster, the BBC clearly recognises the value of its relationship with children and young audiences, and continues to provide wide-ranging children's services … but the return to the "fewer, bigger, better" philosophy mitigates against innovation. Although the Ofcom quota for originations is fulfilled, the pressures on budgets remains – and is likely to increase.

The future of iPlayer Kids and the implications of the merger with BBC Education also need to be considered. Indeed, the future role of the whole BBC, including how it relates to its commercial public service neighbours and the rapidly changing landscape for new, orginal content (and, through that, the loyalty of viewers), is subject to question in an increasingly complex and competitive media world.

Internet safety

Greg Childs mentions *Online Harms* in his introduction. This is a government White Paper, containing comprehensive proposals which comprise both legislative and non-legislative measures both to potentially "regulate" the internet and make companies responsible for their users' safety, especially children and "other vulnerable groups".

It proposes a new regulatory framework and a new independent regulator for online safety, which might well be Ofcom. The regulator will have a range of powers, including the power to impose "substantial fines". There are also proposals to develop a new media-literacy strategy, aimed at both children and adults.

These are certainly important and ground-breaking steps, but they need careful analysis. It is important that a balance remains between protection, and freedom to explore and experiment. CMF has submitted our response; the consultation closed at the beginning of July and there will no doubt be further debate once the results of the consultation are published.

Best possible children's media

I am sure that many other issues will arise during the coming year. We live in a world where things change very quickly, in terms of both politics and media. Whatever happens next, CMF will continue to react, comment, lobby and campaign to ensure the best possible media for UK children.

I would like to thank all our patrons and supporters for their financial support – which is vital. Thanks, too, to our CMF Executive team, who carry out so much of our work. Also, to the CMF Board; to our new Deputy Director, Colin Ward; to Director, Greg Childs; and Administrator, Jacqui Wells, for keeping the organisation alive, alert and ready to react as issues unfold.

SOONER RATHER THAN LATER

5Rights Foundation calls for swifter legislation on internet safety

—

The digital world was imagined as one in which all users would be equal, yet one third of internet users are children. This means that nearly one billion children are growing up in an environment that systematically fails to recognise their age and the protections, privileges, legal frameworks and rights that together constitute the concept of childhood.

5Rights Foundation works towards a digital environment that anticipates the presence, meets the needs and respects the rights of children and young people. Working closely with children,

5Rights operates in the engine room of the digital world: supporting enforceable regulation and international agreements, developing technical standards and protocols, and helping businesses reimagine the design of their digital services.

5Rights believes that children have the right to a digital environment designed to allow them the freedom to explore and engage creatively, knowledgably and fearlessly.

Online Harms White Paper

It is the first duty of government to keep its citizens safe – particularly the vulnerable, which includes children. 5Rights has long campaigned to bring the tech sector in line with every other sector, by mandating that the safety of child users of digital services is a fundamental responsibility of service providers.

5Rights broadly welcomed the government's Online Harms White Paper, as it set out its proposals to introduce a "new system of accountability and oversight for tech companies"; in particular, the statement of Secretary of State, Jeremy Wright MP, who said: "The era of self-regulation for online companies is over. Voluntary actions from industry to tackle online harms have not been applied consistently or gone far enough. Tech can be an incredible force for good and we want the sector to be part of the solution in protecting their users. However, those that fail to do this will face tough action."

5Rights welcomes the power of technology for good and firmly believes that children must be able to access the digital world. But 5Rights asserts that the commercial interests of a small number of powerful companies have been allowed to overlook the rights and needs of children – and, in so doing, they have created a digital environment that does not properly support childhood.

5Rights welcomes the government's decision to pursue a number of the recommendations made in their report "Towards an Internet Safety Strategy", but 5Rights Foundation's Chair Baroness Kidron cautioned:

Baroness Kidron at the CMC 2018

"The issues are so serious, and the failure of the tech sector to self-regulate so profound, that it is incumbent on government to fast-track legislation. I welcome the duty of care, I welcome enforceable terms and conditions – which 5Rights has spent years campaigning for – and I welcome stronger powers to sanction by an independent regulator. But we need all of it swiftly, robustly and uncompromisingly. The real litmus test for this White Paper is whether it results in effective and enforceable legislation, sooner rather than later."

Everyday harms

5Rights remain concerned at the lack of provision to tackle everyday harms, such as compulsion and the use of behavioural designs to push children into actions that are harmful.

Features and techniques that nudge children into activities that are either harmful or habit-forming are ubiquitous in the digital ecosystem, and the harms that emerge need greater attention. Recent concerns about addictive loops of behaviour on gaming, social media and video-sharing platforms have been voiced by the Chief Medical Officer, the NHS and many civil-society groups that work directly with children.

Indeed, the White Paper refers to 5Rights'

report "Disrupted Childhood", which provides an evidence base for the impact of "persuasive design" on children's safety and wellbeing.

These everyday harms – a direct result of the sector's commercial interest in excessive data collection and surveillance – are overlooked for specific intervention in the White Paper. This represents a clear failure by the government to exercise its own duty of care to children, which 5Rights has committed to raising in its response to the consultation.

A new deal

Finally, 5Rights welcomes the government's commitment to the Information Commissioner's Age Appropriate Design Code.

The Code is the first of its kind anywhere in the world, and will require online services to provide specific protection for children's data. The Code offers a first step to changing the status quo, by requiring services to recognise children and childhood, and consider their best interests and needs at different ages.

5Rights believes that the Code will cement a new deal between online services and children. Having introduced an amendment to the Data Protection Act that established the Code, and having been closely involved with its creation and its progress to date, 5Rights has been working closely alongside colleagues and their network to ensure that its implementation is effective and robust.

Further reading

- "Online Harms White Paper", HM Government – assets.publishing. service.gov.uk/government/ uploads/system/uploads/ attachment_data/file/793360/ Online_Harms_White_Paper.pdf

- "Towards an Internet Strategy", 5Rights Foundation – 5rightsfoundation.com/ static/5rights_Towards_an_Internet_ Safety_Strategy_FINAL.pdf

- "Disrupted Childhood: the Cost of Persuasive Design", 5Rights Foundation – 5rightsfoundation. com/static/5Rights-Disrupted-Childhood.pdf

- "Draft Age Appropriate Design Code", Information Commissioner's Office – ico.org.uk/media/about-the-ico/consultations/2614762/ age-appropriate-design-code-for-public-consultation.pdf

- "Briefing on the draft Age Appropriate Design Code", 5Rights Foundation – 5rightsfoundation.com/ uploads/5rightsaadcbriefing.pdf

For further information, visit www.5rightsfoundation.com
To contact 5Rights Foundation, email info@5rightsfoundation.com

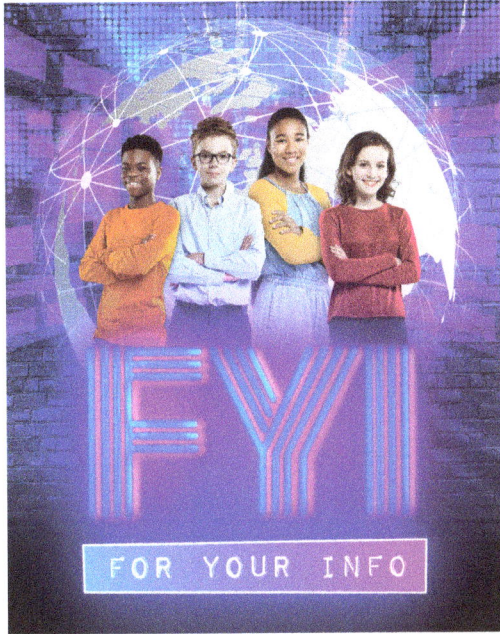

IF CHILDREN RAN THE WORLD

NICKY COX MBE

—

I often muse about what it might be like if children ran the world.

It sounds far-fetched, I'll admit. But, from what I've recently observed, it's no sillier than the idea that our lives and our world are in the hands of politicians, whose biggest priority is the result of the next election. This means that the health of our planet is trapped in the short term.

So: we need kids to save our souls. I always say that children make up 27% of the world's population, but 100% of its future. And, for the world to become a better place, the next generation needs to be better informed than the last.

For the past thirteen years, my children's newspaper – *First News* – has given the children of Britain a voice about the issues that matter most to them. It's not a new idea; indeed, children have an official right to be heard. The United Nation's Convention on the Rights of the Child states:

"When adults are making decisions that affect children, children have the right to say what they think should happen and have their opinions taken into account." And Article 17 states that: "Governments should encourage the media to provide information to children that they can understand."

If recent waves of youth activism are anything to go by, I think we can safely say that our young people understood their rights, but are acting on them, too.

The digital age has made the world a much smaller place and children are passionately engaging with what goes on in it. The internet is often maligned (with good reason) for being the cause of many ill effects on young people. But it has also enabled a new wave of youth activism; an uprising among our youngest citizens.

The most recent examples are the ongoing school-strikes for climate change, inspired by Sweden's Greta Thunberg – who, at 16, has become the world's best known eco-warrior.

One day last summer, aged 15, Greta skipped school, sat down outside the Swedish parliament … and inadvertently kicked off a global movement. "Some people can let things go," she said. "I can't."

On a visit to Britain in April, the teenage Nobel Peace Prize nominee told our politicians:

"My name is Greta Thunberg. I am 16 years old. I come from Sweden. And I speak on behalf of future generations. We children are not sacrificing our education and our childhood for you to tell us what you consider is politically possible in the society that you have created. We children are doing this to wake the adults up. We children are doing this for you to put your differences aside and start acting as you would in a crisis. We children are doing this because we want our hopes and dreams back."

On 15 March, an estimated 1.6 million

students from 125 countries followed Greta's lead and walked out of school to demand climate change action. Now, many are boycotting school every Friday until their countries adhere to the 2015 Paris agreement.

As founder and editor of children's newspaper, *First News*, I have always seen it as my mission to get children's voices heard. That mission has been furthered by *FYI*, a Sky Kids' children's news-show which I co-created with the factual indie production company Fresh Start Media.

From twelve year old Jess Trueman, holding a sit-in at her local library to stop her council closing it down, to the thousands of *First News* readers who helped write the Children's Charter for Brexit, to the boys wearing school-skirts in protest against a uniform policy that wouldn't allow them to wear shorts in hot weather, to the students of Parkland, Florida, protesting with their #NeverAgain movement against gun ownership in America, we champion children's voices.

It has been relatively straightforward up until now. But we have had to think hard about how we write about the school strike for climate change by pupils, particularly when 10,000 schools – and their teachers – use *First News* in the classroom. The ongoing school strikes raise issues of law and safeguarding when children are, in effect, truanting, and not in the care of adults. So, we had to resist the temptation to run with the headline "Great Greta!" and go, instead, with "Greta: 'It's Up To Us'." Our job is to enable Greta, and other young people, to get their voices heard, not to chime in with our own.

These young people speak with their heads and their hearts, because they haven't yet been bewitched by power, money and greed – which have seduced adults. Kids take a longer view; what they see is that we can't put a price on the end of the world.

For all of these reasons, I'd like to see what happened if children ran the world… ○

OUT OF THE MOUTHS OF KIDS:

Francesca (11) on refugees: "These children are the new generation. By giving them a new start you are giving them a new future."

Linus (9) on Brexit: "I love all things British. I love the fish and chips, I love the green hills and I do like a good cream tea, but here's the thing: I don't feel British, I feel European. I feel like I'm part of a world, not just part of one country."

Greta Thunberg (16) on climate change: "You say you love your children above all else, and yet you are stealing their future in front of their very eyes… We cannot solve a crisis without treating it as a crisis … if solutions within the system are so impossible to find, then … we should change the system itself."

CRAZE-Y FOR FORTNITE

STUART DREDGE

—

For many children, the biggest "TV" star to have emerged over the last couple of years isn't actually on TV.

He's a 27 year old American called Tyler Blevins, better known by his online alias: "Ninja". He's been streaming live video of himself playing games since 2011, but his true breakthrough happened in the last 18 months – thanks to a game called *Fortnite*.

Parents (and hopefully, by now, people working in children's media) won't need an introduction to *Fortnite*. The action game's free "Battle Royale" mode launched in September 2017 and by November 2018, *Fortnite* had signed up more than 200

million registered players. How many of those are children is unknown, but it's fair to say that Fortnite was THE gaming craze for children aged eight and up last year.

Like *Minecraft* before it, *Fortnite* has also spawned its own ecosystem of stars – "influencers" – streaming video of their exploits on services like Twitch and YouTube. Ninja is the most prominent: by March 2018, he was breaking live-streaming records playing with music stars Drake and Travis Scott, as well as revealing that his *Fortnite* skills were earning him $500,000 a month.

Ninja's success came as a host of YouTubers popular with children switched their energies from *Minecraft* to *Fortnite*, mirroring (or even catching up to) the habits of their young audiences. *Minecraft* isn't dead by a long shot – it still had more than 91 million active players in October 2018 – but its status as the hottest game for kids has certainly been threatened.

It's not wildly-original to suggest that when children move from one craze to another, it's a swift process. Just ask anyone selling fidget-spinners – if you can find them underneath their mountain of unsold stock!

The parallels between *Fortnite* and *Minecraft*, as well as other digital crazes before them – from *Moshi Monsters* to "surprise egg" unboxing videos on YouTube – are well worth studying by anyone in the world of children's media. Not least because these properties often seem to reach craze status with kids before they're properly on the industry's radar.

They catch us by surprise, and leave us asking "Where did this come from?"

Fortnite - Nintendo Switch

and "How did it get so popular?" – not to mention, "Why are so many children suddenly doing the floss dance in the playground?" By the time we, as an industry, have figured out the answers to these questions, children may well be about to jump to the next thing.

Tracing the roots of digital crazes and understanding the factors driving their popularity is a valuable activity that we could be doing more of, just as we strive to understand the formula for big hits in the worlds of television and publishing. Often, this can teach us important lessons about what the latest generation of digital kids wants from their entertainment.

The narrative-free sandbox of *Minecraft* was a reminder that children wanted to create not just consume, for example. *Fortnite*'s appeal is less about shooting players than it is about a virtual space in which to hang out and chat (and floss). In both cases, we also saw the creation of new stars, from Stampy and DanTDM in the *Minecraft* days to Ninja in the *Fortnite* era. Through these stars, we can understand more about the personalities and content that children want – which don't often match directly with the views of TV commissioners.

But there are other lessons to learn from these digital crazes. Can we spot them coming earlier, rather than getting a shock when they're already massive? Good research, whether from in-house teams or external agencies, has a role to play here. Can we apply some of these lessons to brands coming out of the traditional children's media? It makes sense to at least explore the idea, and in a more nuanced way than simply shoehorning some Creepers into a CBBC show, or making a *Peppa Pig: Battle Royale* game... As much as that last idea may appeal to some parents. ◯

Minecraft - XBox

GAMBLING AND GAMING

What's the difference?

HEATHER WARDLE

—

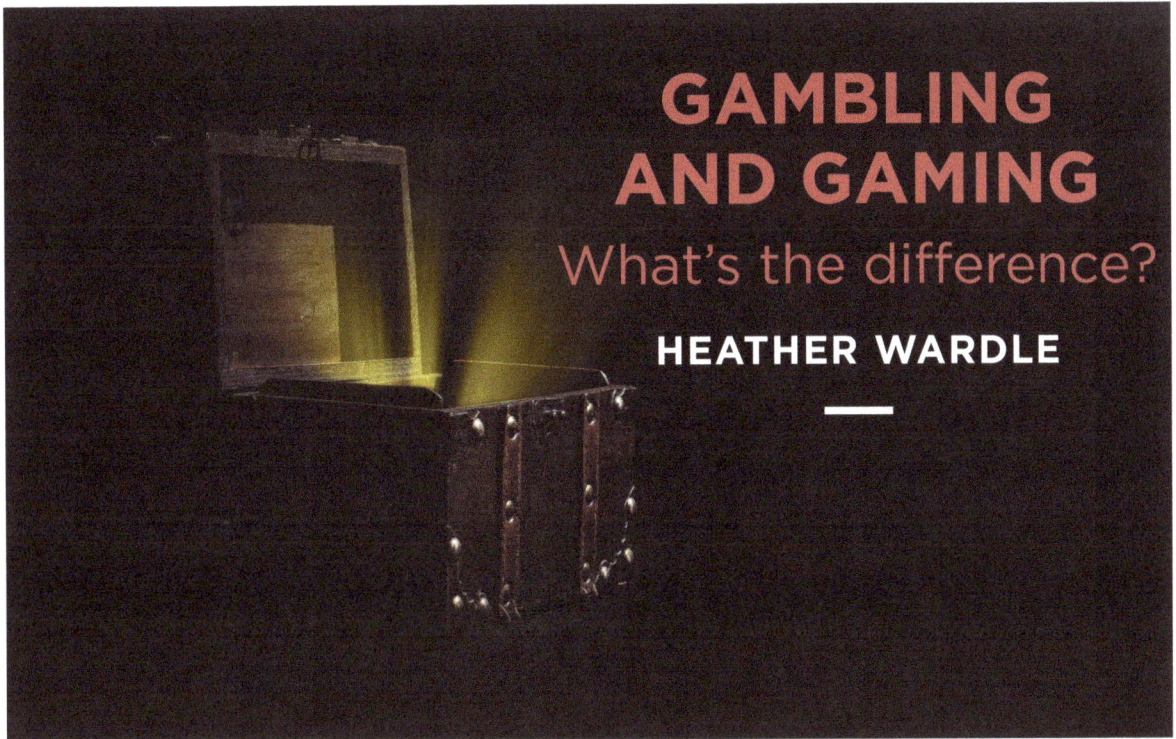

"You don't buy something, you buy the chance to get something" – so said a particularly astute 14 year old boy, when describing loot boxes in video games.

For those of us for whom being a 14 year old is a distant memory, loot boxes are virtual crates in certain video games which players can pay to open in the hope of their containing an item (a weapon, additional power or even just a really attractive digital piece) worth more than the money spent on it. In some respects, they are video games' equivalent of a raffle or tombola; essentially, you are betting on the chance of winning.

Academic and regulatory policy interest has coalesced around loot boxes, and they have been used as examples of the encroachment of gambling activities into everyday life. There is also increasing concern among researchers and regulators about the impact on young people, and talk of the "normalisation of gambling". Mark Johnson's recent research with game-developers has suggested that they are "sleepwalking" into potential problems as they have little awareness of the issues or ethics surrounding loot boxes and gambling.[1]

So, why the concern about loot boxes? First, they have exceptional reach. In Britain it is estimated that 31% of 11 to 16 year olds have paid money within video games to open loot boxes. This sets loot boxes apart from your traditional tombola or raffle at the school fair and

---

1   Johnson, M. "Loot Boxes: a striking new element in the ongoing gamblification of video games." Alberta Gaming Research Institute, Fall Newsletter (2018). Available at: https://prism. ucalgary.ca/bitstream/handle/1880/106824/AGRI_GRRNwslttr_Fall2018.pdf

puts it on an equal, if not excess, footing with children playing the slot machines or buying tickets for the National Lottery. Loot boxes are highly popular products, particularly among boys, which leads to heightened concerns about their potential impact.

Second, they are extractive. The primary purpose of the loot box is a revenue stream for game designers and publishers; they are increasingly essential components of creating profitable games for corporations. Again, this is a far cry from the tombola analogy where the money is circulating and being redistributed (largely) for good causes within a much smaller network.

Finally, the power imbalance between consumer and corporations also raises concerns. This is not a small, closed network of gamers where money passes between friends as, generally, part of a redistributive process (think of the ongoing card games you might have had with your mates at school). This is some large corporations deliberately embedding extractive processes within a large open system – and, in some cases, making buying loot boxes a contingent part of game play. You'll struggle to complete some games if don't buy loot boxes.

A number of academics have focused on the potential impact of embedding these gambling mechanics within video games.[2] Gambling early in life is a known risk factor for subsequent gambling problems. However, we have been here before; there have long been debates about the effects of video games on "real" life behaviours.

For me, the issue is one of power. Gaming corporations are extracting millions of pounds from young consumers through these features. The defining line between gaming and gambling is often held to be whether the game involves profit (gaming theorists have often stated that games are essentially unproductive – everyone finishes as they began, with regard to their material consequences). Loot boxes clearly involve profit: in fact, the primary driver governing their development is profit. This, arguably, moves them away from being simple aspects of game play and towards being considered forms of gambling.

In the UK, nearly all other forms of commercial gambling activity are regulated and subject to age restrictions. Not Loot Boxes. They operate outside of the regulators purview and there are no limitations on who can use them. As we have recently seen from other online content providers, self-regulation is not the best way to protect consumers and perhaps greater regulation of these products is needed, bringing them in line with other standard regulations for commercial gambling activities.

As another 14 year old said:

"Opening a chest in a game is gambling, because you pay for it and you hope you get lucky."[3]

If this is the case then thinking critically about these practices is warranted.. ☉

Heather is Assistant Professor at the London School of Hygiene and Tropical Medicine, and is funded by Wellcome (grant number: 200306/Z/15/Z).

---

2   King, D. and Delfabbro, P. "Predatory monetization schemes in video games (e.g. loot boxes) and internet gaming disorder." Addiction, 113:11, 1967–69 (2018).

3   These quotes were generated by focus groups from a larger project looking at youth gambling harms. See Blake, M., Pye, J., Mollidor, C., Morris, L., Wardle, H. and Reith, G. "Measuring gambling-related harms among children and young people: A framework for action." Ipsos MORI (2019).

SpecialEffect therapists help Finlay play FIFA for the first time.

FINLAY'S DREAM COME TRUE
Beating disability to play video games

—

As children's brands reach out to users across multiple formats, how can we build products that also cater for players with disabilities? Subtitles and audio tracks are commonplace – but when physical disabilities are involved, we need to find innovative solutions...

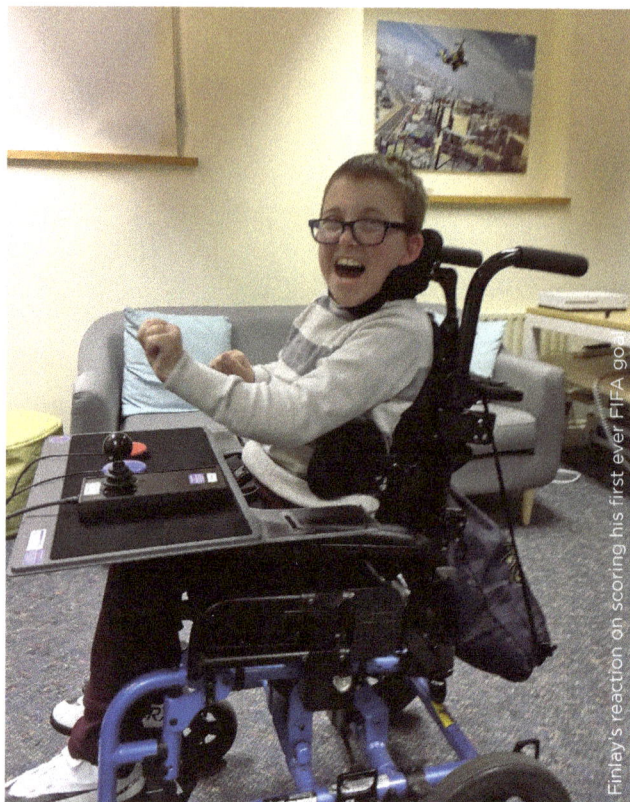

Finlay's reaction on scoring his first ever FIFA goal

Video games facilitate inclusion, friendship, confidence and creativity. But the vast majority of games rely on small, complex handheld controllers or keyboard presses, which require access, dexterity and speed – things that many people with physical disabilities simply can't manage. So they miss out.

Because of his cerebral palsy, Finlay doesn't have the kind of fine hand and finger control needed to use a standard games controller. But he's still able to have a fantastic time playing FIFA with his friends and family, thanks to a custom gaming control setup created by the charity SpecialEffect.

"Thank you for making my dream come true," he said.

Using technology ranging from modified games controllers to eye-control, SpecialEffect, based in the UK, finds ways for people of all ages to play games to the very best of their abilities. There's no one-size-fits-all way of doing this, so they meet people face-to-face to find out exactly what they want to play and what they need to do so. They then match or modify technology to create personalised gaming control setups for loan, and back this up with lifelong follow-up support.

Finlay's fun is also made possible by Electronic Arts, the developers of the FIFA series, who have included a setting that allows the game to be played using only one joystick and two buttons. Originally envisaged as a "Dad Mode", which would encourage non-gaming parents to play with their children, this setting has potentially enabled the game to be enjoyed by countless players with disabilities around the world.

By creating in-game settings and levels that make games easier to play – for example, by providing an alternative way of carrying out tricky controller actions such as button mashing – game developers can make their products inclusive for millions of players who could otherwise only watch others have all the fun.

SpecialEffect collaborates with hardware and software developers to help them consider and build in this kind of accessibility at the start of the game design process. Their freely-available utilities, like the EyeMine software that allows Minecraft to be played with eye movement alone, are bringing the magic of gaming to many thousands more around the globe.

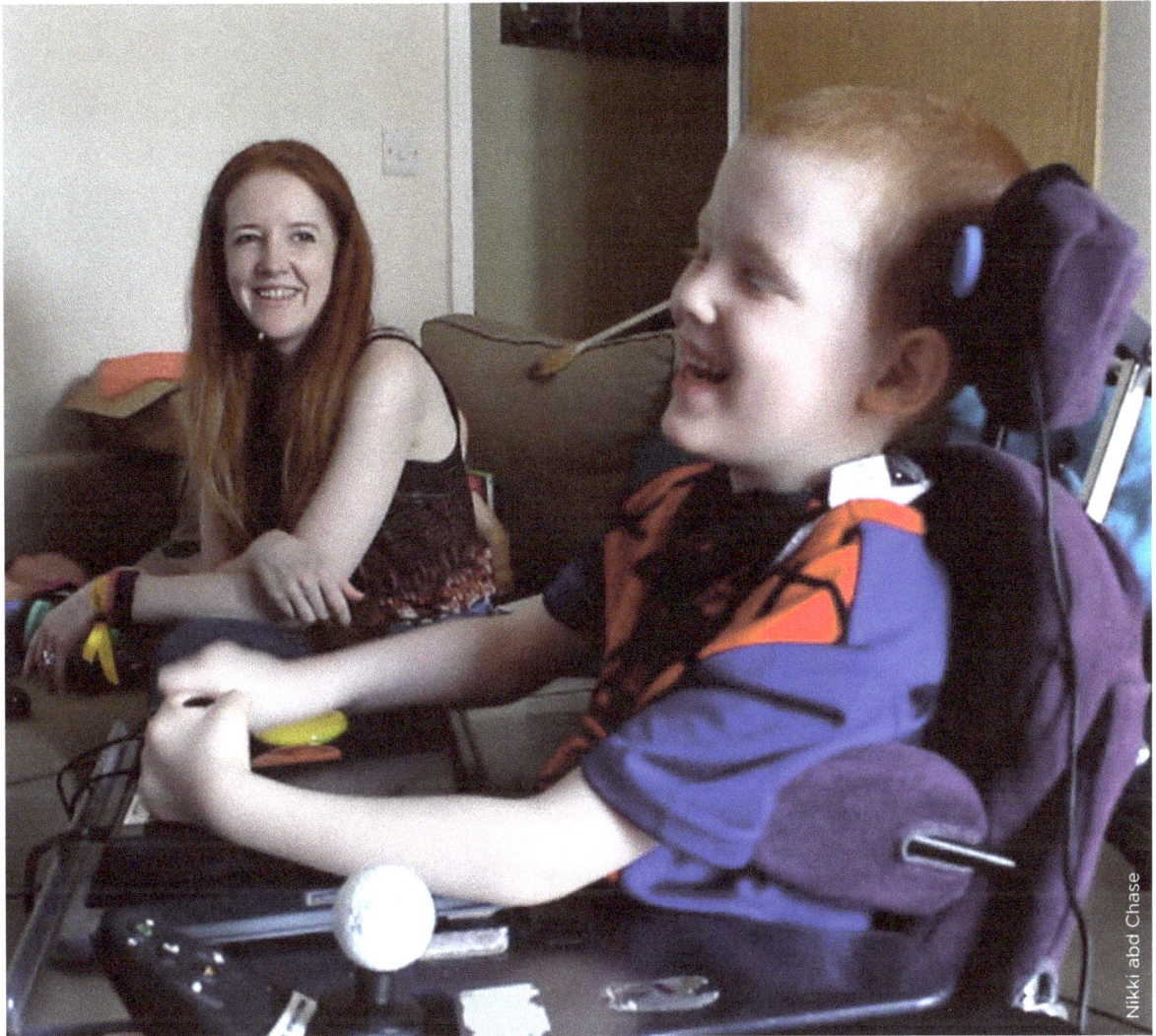

Nikki abd Chase

The impact is life-changing. Nikki, the mum of a young man called Chase whom the charity has helped in a similar way, said,

"We've always been a huge gaming family, so it's something I wanted my children to have the opportunity to do. Particularly for disabled people, I think games are really important – because someone who's able-bodied can go and play golf, they can drive a car, they can do almost anything in real life. Chase isn't going to have those same opportunities, so him being able to play a game creates a level playing field. And as a parent it's made so much difference."

www.specialeffect.org.uk

Finlay's story: www.youtube.com/watch?v=orvn1W15lxM

WHEN WORLDS COLLIDE

Virtual and augmented reality for children: where will it take storytelling?

CANDI BLOXHAM

—

Kirk might call it boldly going, or Alice might see it as stepping through the looking glass, but how ready are we to give kids, the right kind of new reality?

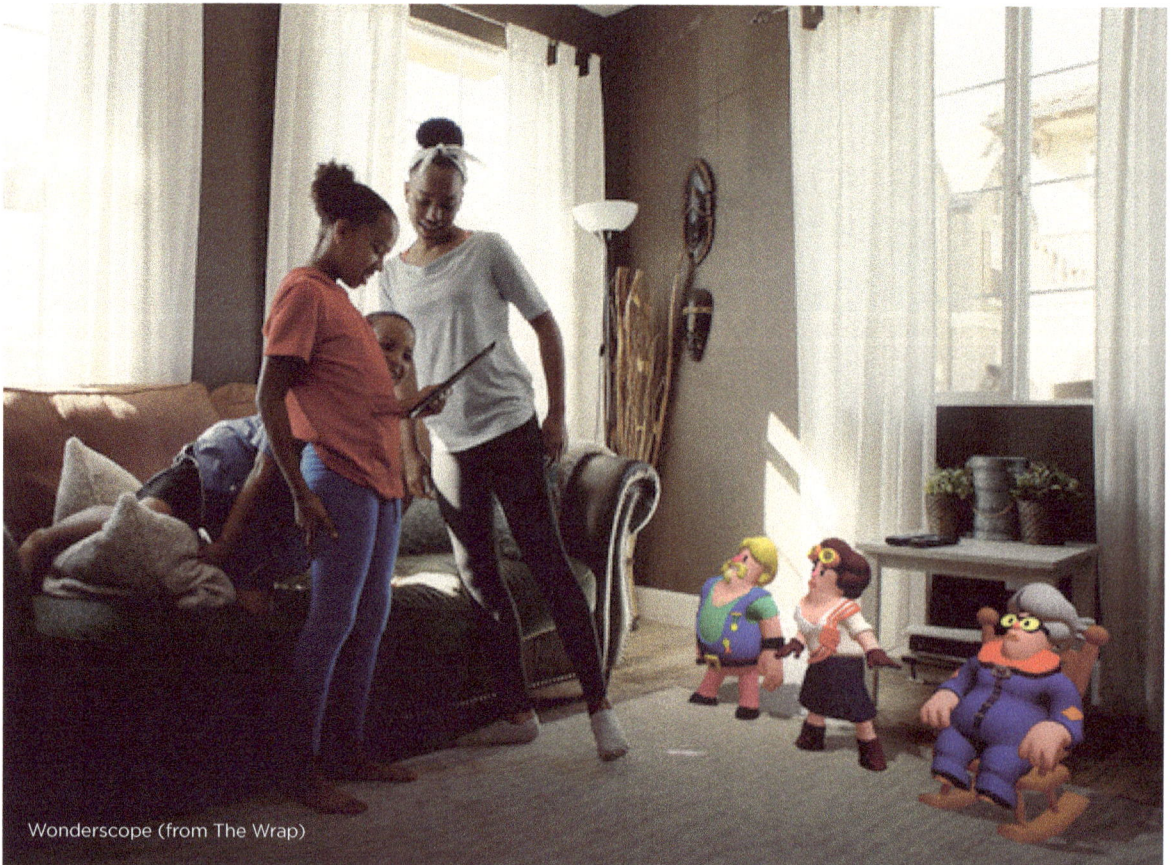

Wonderscope (from The Wrap)

What if the world, your classroom, or living room had more to offer you? What if your favourite characters could always be with you, wherever you are? What if your world and theirs collided into one? Any pre-school kid would love to have Peppa Pig jumping in puddles with them or a haptic Duggee hug. But more than our worlds colliding, don't we all just want to be part of the story?

We need to think beyond technology constraints and adoption, to fully harness these new technologies to take what we offer kids to the next level rather than replicating paper metaphors or purely putting our characters into narrative based games.

VR can fully immerse you in a different time, alternative dimension or a bold new world. AR can bring anything you can imagine to sit alongside the tangible world in which you live and breathe. Extended reality can be a nutritious story experience, starting from the confines of your own home. Suddenly a spaceship will land on the unmade bed and aliens will cascade down the curtains, turning an otherwise normal setting into an extraordinary storyscape. Before you have time to switch off, the narrative starts: those aliens are hunting monsters you never knew lived under your bed. There is a call to action: whose side are you on? Before we know it, we are not only immersed in the story, but are a protagonist who can effect change in this bedroom battleground.

Immersive storytelling should not only visually excite us, but move away from being a passive, linear narrative to allow for active engagement with the unfolding drama. This tends to follow models from the gaming industry. The success of MMO (Massive Multiplayer Online) and sandbox games such as *Minecraft* and more recently *Fortnite*, show the massive demand for community based, world building experiences, which we can share with friends and where we can not only play a game but invest in the same narratives.

The challenge will be to move beyond the passive to offer a quality immersive storytelling experience but avoid becoming simply another gaming arena. Wonderscope have shown some interesting examples of

Fortnite - Epic

storytelling on this platform, where their ambitions have been to enable the audience to live the story not just observe it. There are indications that industry leaders in the storytelling field are breaking new ground in this area. Aardman, as part of a consortium of British companies, recently announced that it will bring out an "immersive experience" based on the *Wallace & Gromit* characters. The platform will feature augmented reality with multiplayer action, but with what promises to be narrative driven content.

As with all new technologies, the first examples of extended reality for the children's market have been limited, even gimmicky, but the possibilities are like an under-discovered utopian world. The lines dividing the viewing platforms are fading. We have a wonderful opportunity to extend our stories, make new ones, and bring the audience even closer to characters and their worlds with active, non-linear narrative. We've all seen *Ready Player One*. It doesn't have to be an escape from reality but a tool to improve it. What if we use extended reality stories to teach STEM in the classroom? To bring children from different backgrounds, even countries, to one place where they can experience the same narrative and join in together. To help preschoolers understand colours and numbers through characters and stories set in the real world? To step into the shoes of a bullied teen in a *Grange Hill* style drama, to help with emotional decisions and resilience?

It's about finding the balance, between the narrative, the interaction, and the cool stuff. To make something of worth that goes beyond the gimmick, the game or a marketing tool. But how do we get there? By being brave, taking risks and asking questions. By going boldly through the looking glass.

Let's take our shows, characters and stories to the next level! ▶

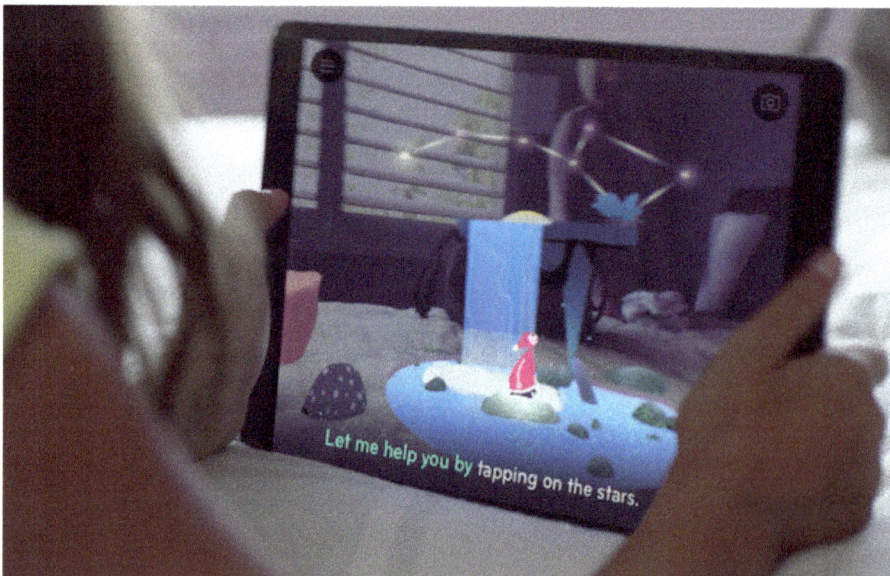

Little Red - Wonderscope
(from The Wrap)

CLICKS AND MORTAR
Unravelling the new retail landscape

TESSA MOORE AND JULIET TZABAR

—

"Retail is Dead – Long Live E-tail!"
"Death of the UK High Street!"

Over the last couple of years, this type of headline has become daily reading. Combined with either the closure of chains or a reduction in store numbers across many household names – including TRU, Maplin, House of Fraser, Debenhams, Evans, Mothercare and even Marks & Spencer – there appears to be general agreement that consumer-shift to online buying, and the dominance of Amazon in particular, is a key-driver of this decline.

There is no doubt that traditional retail is challenged as consumer habits shift to digital. We now enjoy all kinds of household activities – from watching TV or a film to reading the news, listening to music, socialising and shopping – through our mobiles, laptops or voice-activated tech. But what does that mean for the children's entertainment industry and licensed brands? While the plethora of content platforms can only be good news, how has this shift affected smaller producers or creators of kids' properties, who have not managed to secure a suite of licensing partners but know they have a strong following?

Well, it's not all doom and gloom! The traditional licensing market remains strong (with a global value of $270bn and NPD reporting 25% of those unit sales were children's product). However, the squeeze on shelf space sees it dominated by the big blockbuster brands, from the big blockbuster studios with even bigger blockbuster budgets! Toy companies that are now investing in their own content arms also have deep pockets and better leverage to commandeer space, both locally and globally.

This makes it very hard for an indie producer to gain any sort of real traction in consumer products through the traditional routes. But the good news is that there are opportunities out there, and – as you would expect from our tenacious and creative industry – there are businesses and IP owners bent on exploring the increasingly important world of selling direct to consumers, through digital platforms and particularly social media.

E-commerce and direct-to-consumer (DTC) is a huge success story in many sectors, often due to a very different approach to marketing. Thanks to the growth in Facebook and Instagram, in particular, opportunities for smaller companies are skyrocketing. While Facebook remains the dominant platform (90% of social media use in the UK; source: TrackMaven), Instagram is making huge strides, particularly with the millennial audience – and many of these Gen Y-ers are young parents and … toy-buyers! According to Hootsuite, 72% of Instagram users have bought a product directly from the platform and the growth in "shoppable posts" has made it easier for the channel owner to sell, and the consumer to buy, directly from the source.

Jules Coke, CEO of Doodle Productions has recently opened a dedicated online shop to support their successful preschool TV series *Messy Goes to Okido*, broadcast on CBeebies since 2015 and based on the popular STEAM-focused *Okido* magazine. The store was created in-house to sustain the brand look and feel; it offers a wide range of products, with all marketing and distribution handled in-house. Commenting on the decision to "do it themselves", Coke said, "The traditional licensing model doesn't work for us – or about 98% of other kids' brands. By opening our own store, we give our audience what they want and have full global control over our brand."

The popular creator of award-winning preschool apps, Sago Mini, was purchased by fellow Canadian toy giant Spinmaster in 2016. Their 16 apps have been downloaded over 13 million times. Sago Mini also cited brand control as one of the reasons they decided to invest in their own product development team; they are trialling different routes to market for their consumer products, including specialist retail and dedicated online retailers. CEO Jason Krogh says, "The central challenge I'm interested in is how to create profitable consumer products businesses for brands with smaller but super passionate fans. With media consumption quickly fracturing I see this as the real opportunity going forward."

In practical terms, there are many sites offering the chance for smaller or nascent properties, which allow you to assess demand, create an "official" site and also avoid any potential cannibalisation or infringement of your IP. Do-it-yourself Print on Demand sites, such as Shopify, Redbubble and Fine Art America, allow you to create artwork, upload it and choose between a set of templates to create the product you want, from clothing to posters to gifts. The site manages sales fulfilment and as the "artist" you get commission on sales without any of the financial investment in inventory, shipping etc.

Clients include the phenomenal *Tiana of Toys AndMe* YouTube fame, who has picked up over 15 million subscribers across her channels in just two years.

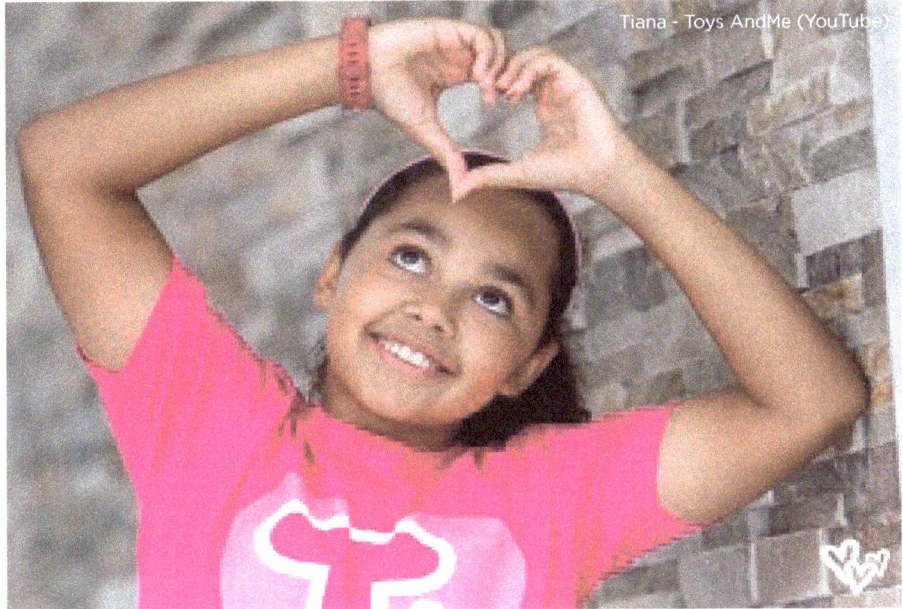
Tiana - Toys AndMe (YouTube)

For digital-first brands with a direct channel to the consumer, the opportunity to sell through social media is significant – but with kid-targeted brands, the landscape can be hard to navigate. The Viral Talent Agency is a full-service influencer agency, which works with both brands and influencers to maximise results for both parties. Expertise in this area is vital: both to ensure that you keep within regulatory environment and, equally importantly, cultivate parental approbation without alienating the audience. "It is important that your social commerce strategies are an extension of the brand experience you are already offering, and everything we handle in the kid space has to be family-friendly," says Laura Edwards, Viral's Co-Founder.

The social media channels may not currently be an easy or familiar world for many in the industry, but the direct connection with your audience, the retention of a higher margin and the creative control of your products, make it an attractive option. There is a continued degree of risk, but even a small sales success could help drive the profitability of your brand and secure its future.

And who knows … you may also attract the attention of a global partner!

DOWN THE RABBIT HOLE
Immersive journeys in education
BECKY JONES

The time for immersive learning has come. Long teetering on the edge of possibility, are VR and AR finally coming into their own? What is the potential for immersive learning in schools? Can the newer skills of gamification and transmedia storytelling make an impact across the education space? How important will they be to the next generation?

The theme of this year's Children's Media Conference is "Limitless" – defined, variously, as "without end" and "boundless". Children are limitless by nature; they are curious, determined, imaginative and hungry for knowledge. Children also like to be entertained. What we give them, how we feed their imaginations and keep them wanting more, has never been more important. The question is, how can we create and deliver the kind of things that they will most engage with?

This is perhaps even more important in education, where children can be switched on to learning through the classroom experience. It's also big business: every year, UK schools spend £900 million on education technology.

When I was at school, video content was not necessarily part of a lesson plan. Watching television was something that required marshalling and organisation at a fixed time every week. A giant machine on a stand was ceremoniously wheeled into the hall, while we all filed in to sit in rows on the floor to gaze up at the box. Only rarely were connections made between what we saw on the big screen, and the chalk and talk that followed once playtime was over.

As we all know, that's changed. Using video as a learning tool has morphed exponentially through education content platforms, both online and via apps. But while technologies such as augmented reality (AR) and virtual reality (VR) have been around for a while, schools are only just beginning to realise their full value and potential. To stay ahead of the game, more education content providers are going to have to upgrade from being short-form video producers to thinking more roundly about the whole learning package by injecting their content with some of the newest technology.

Some key principles of learning will never go away: storytelling, drummed into me from my early days as a producer on the BBC's *Horizon* series, will always be the key to conveying complex information in the most engaging way. What's changed are the tools we can now use to do that. But how well are producers delivering what schools want?

There's new funding for this new thinking and scores of players vying to supply it. Companies such as Inspyro are producing AR and VR content for schools, to bring the pages of books to life or take children on a journey through the trenches of the First World War. Roman soldiers now rise out of history books, wielding their swords to the delight of 8 year olds. Viking warships are constructed in 3Dand you can explore inside a Saxon hut. A company called Curiscope has invented T-shirts for children to wear, which generate images from inside the human body – much to

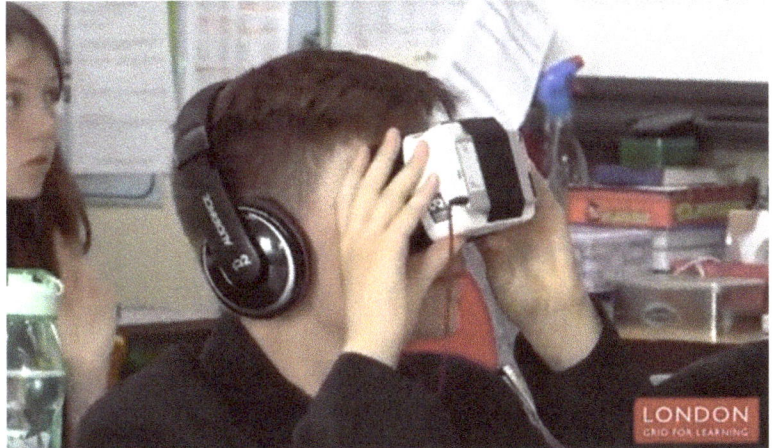

the entertainment of fellow classmates. Even Eric Carle's classic *The Very Hungry Caterpillar* has gone digital: in AR form, kids can feed the caterpillar and watch as he grows, then turns into a butterfly.

VR and 360° allow teachers to take children to places they could never otherwise visit: to soar above the Amazon rainforest or explore an Egyptian tomb. VR and other immersive technologies have also been transformative for children with special needs, for example in allowing autistic children to adapt to a new environment or stimuli gradually, becoming used to it in a controlled setting. Interestingly, schools can use VR in cross-curricular ways, too – including to provide triggers to inspire creative writing, by

Can we broaden the learning experience from the classroom to the wider world by embracing the idea that education can come from all directions and is holistic – that it's not just about passing exams?

No doubt, as we dive further down the rabbit hole, there will be more opportunities for educators and those who make digital content to create better and more imaginative learning experiences. But it is not just about technology. There are whole new ways of putting content together by using the techniques of transmedia storytelling, rolling subjects out across multiple platforms to maintain a child's interest and ensure their engagement through more active participation. Or by introducing gamification techniques, to make sure children stay curious about the world around them and get the most out of learning content.

immersing children in a different world and asking them to write about their experiences. Just watching the reactions of children after VR experiences demonstrates how much they gain from them.

But while VR innovators such as Google Expeditions, with its cardboard viewers and simple technology, have brought virtual field-trips to the classroom, complete VR domination has stalled. Working out exactly what to do with it and how to integrate it into learning has proved a challenge – and issues with cost, and so access to kit and equipment, have prevented scores of schools from adopting VR on the scale once envisaged. Simpler, easier-to-access AR seems to be stealing VR's thunder.

The potential for learning in today's world really is limitless. Children can find out about absolutely anything they want, from almost anywhere. But what do they actually need? What *should* they be learning? And what are the best ways to get that information to them in the future?

We've come a very long way since the television in the school hall. Fifty years ago this July, children all over the world filed into school halls to watch grainy black and white images of the moon landing. Today, the next generation of children may not be any closer to visiting the moon in person – but they can *still* take off in a rocket and fly through space. Virtually, at least. ◉

OXYGEN FOR THE SOUL

VICKY IRELAND MBE FRSA

—

There is a crisis in Arts Education in primary schools.
Did you know? Do you care?

We are currently a society whose movers and shakers are preoccupied with Brexit. Children come low on any agenda and while decisions are being delayed, our children are growing – and the arts are being eroded from their lives in an alarming way. They only have one chance at childhood and it should have, at its centre, a rich and balanced education which includes the arts.

Why? Because the arts provide oxygen for the soul and are the principal trainers of the imagination. Hence the urgency of our proposal of an arts entitlement for every UK child: The Arts Backpack.

The Arts Backpack UK offers every primary-school child access to at least five quality participatory or passive arts experiences a year. These experiences will be collected in a digital backpack, which will serve as a reflection point for the student throughout the school year.

We launched the idea of an Arts Backpack UK in August 2018 at the National Theatre. Speakers at the event included representatives from BAFTA, the European Parliament, Centre for Young Musicians and Shaper/Caper Dance Company. The idea is championed by a number of our illustrious

CBeebies' Chris Jarvis; BAFTA Young Presenter Tianna Moore; Vicky Ireland.

Fife, East Anglia, the South-West and the North-East to coordinate concurrent pilots for the 2019–20 academic year. A future pilot is also in the pipeline for Northern Ireland, who were heavily involved with planning and funding the Feasibility Study.

The aims of the pilots are:

patrons, including Philip Pullman, Jacqueline Wilson and Jenny Agutter, who made the following remark:

> "The 'arts' may reflect our society, or stir the imagination but unless we can relate to them on a fundamental level they will not become a part of our lives. The Arts Backpack might be the needed bridge."

Following this enthusiastic response, we commissioned a Feasibility Study which was published in early 2019 and presented at the Young Vic What Next? Chapter. The study recommended coordinating a number of pilots across the UK, choosing pilot-regions that reflect the various challenges of urban, rural and coastal areas, as well as the different curricula in England, Scotland, Wales and Northern Ireland.

We are currently working with arts organisations, schools and investors in

1. To discover and overcome the challenges of different UK regions. This could be anything from the cost of transporting children to the theatre to persuading parents that cultural activity is worthwhile. (Or it could be something we haven't anticipated!)

2. To create an Arts Backpack scheme that works for teachers. Ideally, the scheme would not add to their workload but offer them the opportunity to develop skills and confidence when teaching arts subjects – something we have repeatedly heard is neglected in teacher training.

3. To consult with children and use their voices and opinions, exploring the idea and function of

a Children's Arts Council in every school.

4. To finesse a safe digital platform where children can store their experiences and share them with their teachers and families.

5. To identify the most effective and sustainable funding models across the UK for future arts-accessibility schemes.

Anyone previously acquainted with Action for Children's Arts will know that we are a small national charity, with big ambitions for every child to have a sense of cultural entitlement. The Arts Backpack UK is an opportunity for us to bring these ambitions to life, to grow as an organisation, and to collaborate with inspirational colleagues across the culture and education sectors. We cannot wait to meet the children, teachers, parents, performers, creatives and administrators who will play a vital part in bringing the pilots to life.

It only costs £2.50 to support our work. Visit childrensarts.org.uk/join/individual to find out more.And please contact mimi.doulton@childrensarts.org.uk if you would be interested in getting involved. ◌

Website: www.childrensarts.org.uk
Twitter: @childrensarts

"I believe that the Arts Backpack idea could be the most significant notion and possibility to have surfaced in the twenty years or more since our charity began"
ACA President, David Wood OBE

Jenny Agutter at the 2016 JM Barrie Awards

WHAT A WONDERFUL SPONGE!

SpongeBob's 20th anniversary

MARC CECCARELLI AND VINCENT WALLER

—

It's crazy to think that this year we're celebrating the 20th anniversary of one of the most iconic TV series and characters ever created, *SpongeBob SquarePants* – and what an incredible ride our little sponge has had. SpongeBob has cemented his status as a pop culture phenomenon, global household name and evergreen franchise that continues to resonate with a multigenerational audience.

The show has reigned continuously as the number-one kids' animated series on TV for the last 17 years and now airs across 208 countries in 55 different languages. We're proud that the *SpongeBob* franchise now boasts 12 seasons, numerous pop culture catchphrases and memes, two theatrical releases, a vast consumer products range worth $13 billion in global sales and a Tony Award-winning Broadway musical – not to mention a huge global fan base!

Back in 1994, when creator Stephen Hillenburg first started formulating the idea for the show, he wanted to make something that stood out from other popular cartoons of the time and was "fantastic but believable". As a marine biologist, Steve wanted to create a small town underwater where the characters were more like humans than fish, with a focus on one particular character: a sea sponge. What eventually ensued was a show that struck a timeless chord with its escapist comedic style, unpredictable, diverse and iconic characters, and universal themes of humour, fun and positivity.

SpongeBob SquarePants has definitely evolved over the years, both in the way it looks and sounds. Visually, the character models in the first three seasons differ from what you see onscreen now as our artists were exploring various ways to draw these characters – and they all interpreted them slightly differently! We could watch episodes from earlier seasons and identify which person story boarded each one. With the development of the first movie, Steve encouraged and trained teams to lock down the models. When we came on board as co-showrunners in 2015, we made the decision to bring back more physical comedy, more setups and punchlines, and bigger emotive reactions from *SpongeBob*'s characters, as a lot of the humour stems from the drawings themselves. A key factor for us has always been to infuse personality and depth into the characters, and stay away from predictability – to keep the look fresh and the audience laughing.

The voice cast has been equally vital to the show's ongoing development and success. Just like the animators, the voice actors have evolved over the years as they've figured out who their characters are, inside and out. It's a highly collaborative process with the voice actors, who continuously read our stories and give feedback on whether the scripts and storylines are authentic to the characters. In the past few years, we've moved Tom Kenny (voice of SpongeBob) into voice directing as well, which has been an amazing asset. He is laser focused on his storyboards and ensures that we are truly representing SpongeBob's mind as he goes through all the different

"We think it's able to cross that boundary for several reasons, including its chemistry-rich cast, storyboard artists and animators, but also, and most importantly, the show's comedy-centric nature. We're mindful to never condescend to our audience and we write the comedy from an honest place"

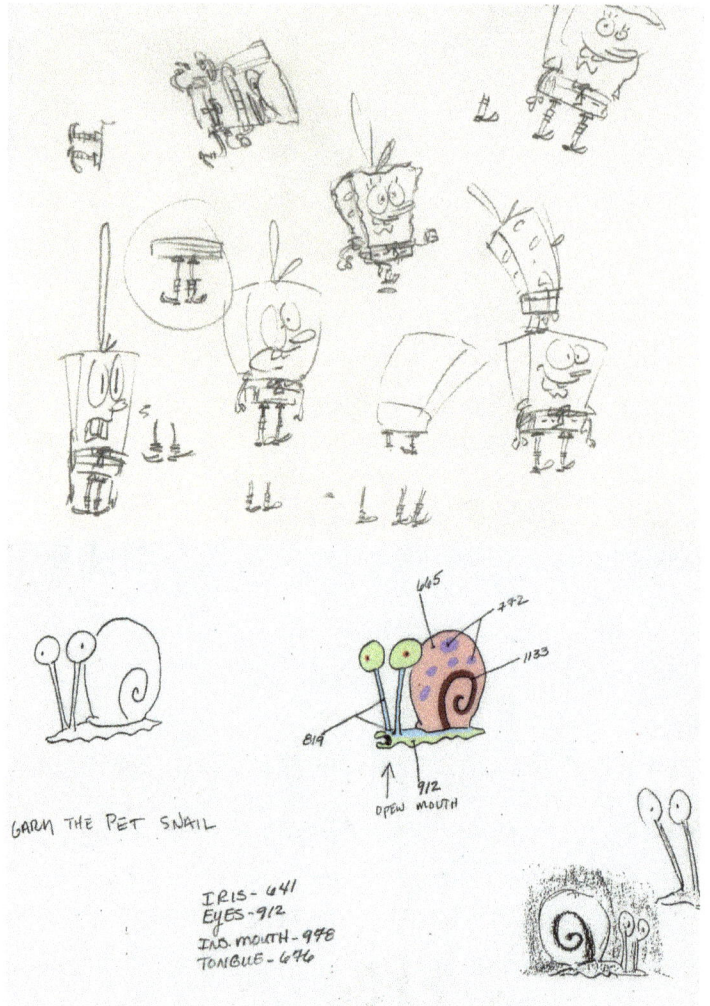

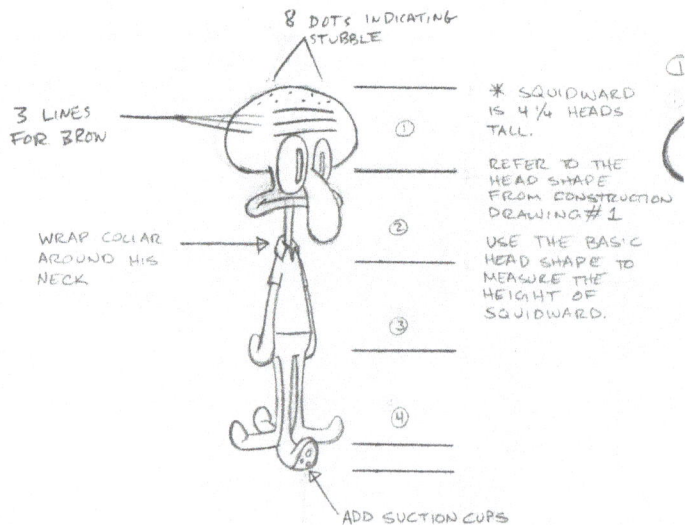

GARY THE PET SNAIL

IRIS - 641
EYES - 912
INS. MOUTH - 998
TONGUE - 696

645
792
1133
814
912
OPEN MOUTH

8 DOTS INDICATING STUBBLE

3 LINES FOR BROW

WRAP COLLAR AROUND HIS NECK

* SQUIDWARD IS 4 1/4 HEADS TALL.

REFER TO THE HEAD SHAPE FROM CONSTRUCTION DRAWING #1

USE THE BASIC HEAD SHAPE TO MEASURE THE HEIGHT OF SQUIDWARD.

ADD SUCTION CUPS

story scenarios. When everybody is creatively on board to make the show as funny as it can possibly be, that's when the magic happens!

So what is it about SpongeBob and his friends in Bikini Bottom that help them endure the test of time? The show's success and appeal to a diverse, broad audience continue to amaze us; in particular SpongeBob's ability to attract an older audience, which is unusual for a show aimed at children. We think it's able to cross that boundary for several reasons, including its chemistry-rich cast, storyboard artists and animators, but also, and most importantly, the show's comedy-centric nature. We're mindful to never condescend to our audience and we write the comedy from an honest place. Viewers don't tune in to SpongeBob for anything but entertainment, so the comedy is more important to us than underlying moral messaging or subtexts. We simply write what makes us and our fans laugh. The only consistent message of the show comes organically from SpongeBob's character – he has a giant heart and tries his best to make Bikini Bottom a great place for every creature who lives there.

The characters and their various personality traits and flaws also appeal to different types of people. SpongeBob SquarePants uniquely takes place in an "adult" world, giving way to more variety in the kinds of stories we can tell and the subject matters we can delve into. SpongeBob has an adult job and adult responsibilities, but he has a kid's heart.

We've met many adult fans at signings who have thanked us profoundly for making an animated show they can laugh along to with their kids.

This year, Nickelodeon is going big to celebrate SpongeBob SquarePants' 20th anniversary. We're launching exciting new long- and short-form episodes and specials – including an hour-long mixed live action and animation SpongeBob birthday episode, featuring the voice cast playing human versions of their characters – a new mobile game and a dedicated YouTube channel. In the retail space, Nickelodeon is collaborating with designers, brands, artists and other SpongeBob fans to debut a new global toy line and limited edition products across all categories. The celebrations will culminate in a new Paramount Pictures and Nickelodeon Movies theatrical release, premiering the summer of 2020 – The SpongeBob Movie: It's a Wonderful Sponge.

As we gear up for this milestone anniversary, we're reminded of how blessed we are that we found our way to SpongeBob and became a part of his journey. This yellow sponge has totally taken over and, in this landscape of children's entertainment, we can't imagine working on any other show. Steve's legacy lives on through his universe of beloved characters and will undoubtedly continue to do so for many more years to come. ◯

Axel Scheffler

FROM "GRRR" TO GLOBAL GRUFFALO

BELINDA IONI RASMUSSEN

—

As Macmillan Children's celebrates 20 years of The Gruffalo, Belinda Ioni Rasmussen reflects on the publishing of author Julia Donaldson and illustrator Axel Scheffler's classic.

Julia says, "I intended the book to be about a tiger, but I just couldn't get anything to rhyme with 'tiger'. It just wasn't working. But then I came up with,Silly old fox, doesn't he know / there's no such thing as a *blank-blank-oh*?' Then I began with '*Grrr*', which I hoped would sound quite scary. Then, all I needed was a word of three syllables ending in 'oh'. Somehow, 'gruffalo' came to mind."

The word "gruffalo" made Axel think of a buffalo, so first he drew him with horns and a tail, walking on all fours. Then he decided the creature should stand up, but his editor still thought he looked too scary. There was clearly a challenge at the time between coming up with a creature that was scary enough to be a monster, but not terrifying – getting the balance right.

The mouse and the Gruffalo were wearing clothes in one of the first sketches. At one stage, the mouse was even wearing lederhosen – but Julia was adamant from the beginning that it was about animals in their natural surroundings.

The Gruffalo was first published by Macmillan in 1999. Everyone knew from the beginning that it had the potential to become a timeless classic, but I am not sure anyone saw the potential extent of the brand to grow beyond the books, at that time. It certainly didn't have a 360 degree brand-approach, as many properties have today from the moment they are conceived. But then, those were different times.

I joined Pan Macmillan as Executive Publisher of Macmillan's Children's Books in 2012. Five years ago, I asked an outside consultant to come in and speak to the team about the licensing market. He kicked off his presentation stating that we were a top-five licensing publisher, which changed our way of thinking. In our minds, we were always picture-book and fiction publishers – but now we had the confidence that our books could compete strongly in the licensing market because of *The Gruffalo*.

Mouse

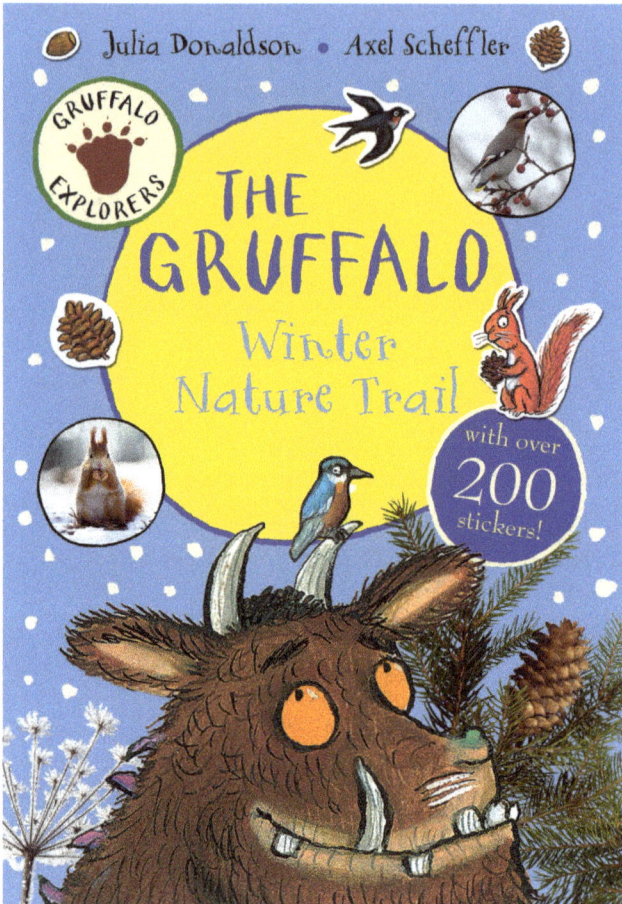

It encouraged us to be more experimental in our product development, though at all times with Julia's and Axel's approval, of course. We work very closely with our authors and illustrators, and consider them part of the team that brings a new book to market; they are part of the process, not just the beginning. Previously, the creative process around *The Gruffalo* had worked nearly exclusively from the idea of a format to a new edition. (I.e. if touch-and-feel books were particularly popular in the market, the story of *The Gruffalo* would be put into a touch-and-feel format if everyone approved.) Now we are less interested in innovative formats and more focused on what *The Gruffalo* stands for, trying to understand the values the consumer attaches to this character.

This is how the idea of the Gruffalo Explorers came about, one of the favourite spin-off publishing series – a series of nature-spotters' guides. They tap into Axel and Julia's own love of nature and the outdoors, and feel like a very natural (no pun intended!) fit for the picture book, with its "deep dark wood" setting and woodland characters. Julia also loves *The Gruffalo* cookbook, where you can learn how to make Gruffalo crumble. Again, the idea is on brand; a natural extension from the allusions to animal recipes in the story.

The other change was that we started focusing more on the consumer, moving from the audience in – ensuring we had books for every age, from babies to experience and grandparents to purchase, for every occasion and touching as many price points as possible.

We have sold 13.5 million copies of *The Gruffalo* worldwide (paperback, hardback and board book), and it has been translated into

Julia Donaldson in India

82 languages, including the north and south dialects of the Sami language and Kolsch, which is spoken around Cologne. German-speaking markets are key because of Axel, and in those the publishing is as developed as in the UK with films, stage-shows and even a Gruffalo opera supporting the brand. The Gruffalo is also very popular in France and China, and last year sold 100,000 copies in the USA.

The fact that Julia and her husband Malcolm, a leading paediatrician, have toured the country performing The Gruffalo directly to children at many different venues has definitely had an influence on awareness and sales too. When Julia and Malcolm go on tour, which happens regularly, we immediately see a significant spike in sales in the relevant country. They recently went to India and travelled from Delhi to Kolkata and onwards to Mumbai and Jaipur, performing to thousands of children. Julia is really quite unique in the energy and commitment she puts into promoting her books. She is unstoppable when it comes to reaching out to her audience, and it's in the good old-fashioned way of being there in person.

Part of *The Gruffalo*'s appeal is that it is a proper fairy tale, and doesn't rely on the reflexive "pro-social" correctness that can afflict children's literature. Everyone loves a David and Goliath story – and a not-too-scary monster is always popular in children's stories, too. Moreover, reading The Gruffalo is a shared experience: adults like it as much as children. There is something nearly therapeutic about the rhyming and the repetition in the book, when read out loud, and Axel's illustrations and attention to detail are, of course, just perfect and a masterpiece on their own.

People so often underestimate what it takes to write a good picture-book story, and how difficult it is to get a story with a plot and a message to fit 32 pages. I argued recently on a panel that *The Gruffalo* has depth. It is about so much more than a courageous mouse. It is about finding your self-confidence and resilience, to battle on when the world is telling you that you are just a mouse. At the same time, it is a funny, simple story You can read it in many different ways. Very few authors and illustrators have succeeded in pulling off this level of sophistication in a picture-book story. ☺

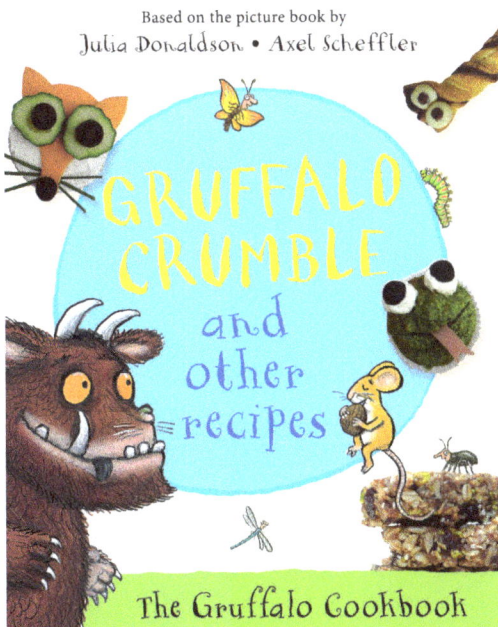

Based on the picture book by
Julia Donaldson • Axel Scheffler

GRUFFALO CRUMBLE and other recipes

The Gruffalo Cookbook

TWICE IN A BLUE MOON

DANIEL POSTGATE

—

On the 50th anniversary of *The Clangers*, Daniel Postgate ponders
the reinvention of his father's classic TV series.

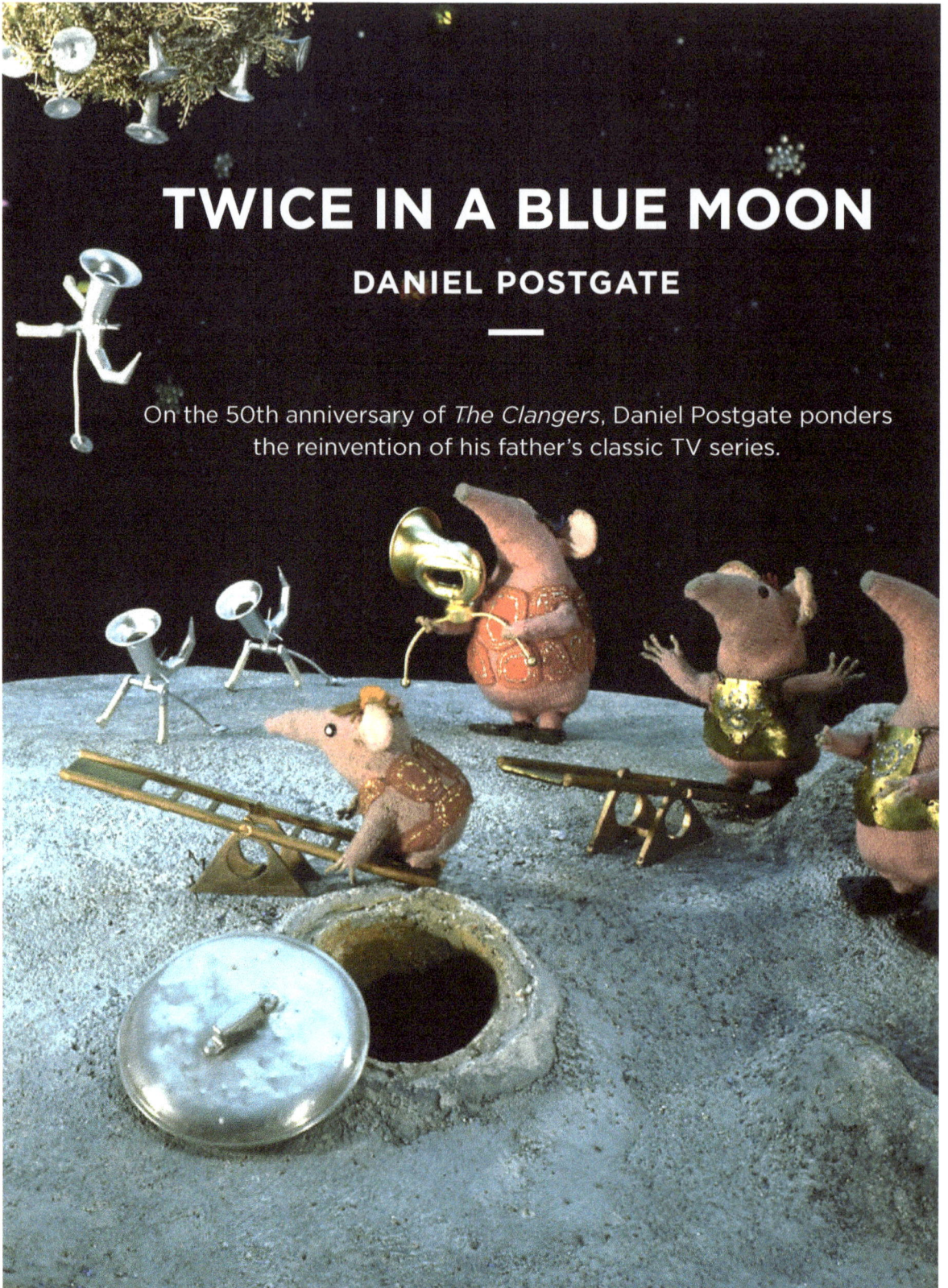

When arriving at the big barn to start a day's shooting, the first thing my father Oliver Postgate did was sponge the bird poo from the surface of the Clangers' planet. Swallows were nesting somewhere high up in the darkness, above ancient beams, and they cared nothing for '70s children's TV. On one occasion, filming was delayed when Oliver discovered mice had nibbled at the Soup Dragon's hand and found it necessary to cross the yard to the cow shed to speak to Peter Firmin, over a cup of tea, about possible solutions.

Late 1960s development sketch by Peter Firmin

When the *Clangers* series was finally finished and in the can, that's when I stepped in. An excited seven year old, I'd carry the retired puppets out into the yard of the Firmins' farm and set them up in tableau – come to Earth on some unspecified mission. I'd lay down, my cheek on the gravel, eyeing them at Clanger-height.

Forty years later, the gravel at my cheek is now the studios of Factory Transmedia in Altrincham, a wonderland of cutting-edge technology. Peter and I push through black curtains into various illuminated scenes, where Clangers go about their curious lives once again. No swallows or mice this time

– it's a tight ship of finely-tuned schedules, across multiple sets and time-frames. Up to six Major Clangers can be busy at any one time, on a multitude of sets. A small army of animators, model makers and directors bustle about. Where Peter's wife Joan once single-handedly knitted the Clanger skins, now there's a dedicated team of knitters. However the ultimate result remains something fairly similar to before, and that's the way everyone involved wants it – charmingly realised stories about a close-knit family.

Peter and I have teamed up with Coolabi, a media company who have lovingly developed the new series and raised finance to make it possible in the scary world of modern TV. They convinced Kay Benbow at CBeebies that it's a good idea to revisit the little blue planet, so it's full steam ahead!

There were ideas about certain changes: the Clangers might have become different colours, like extraterrestrial Teletubbies, and the Froglets a variety of shapes. I thought about including a pair of cheeky woodlouse-like helpers for Major, called Copper-bugs. But in the end, it was considered better to keep things much the same. We did bring in a few tweaks… There was a darkness in the original series – the dark of infinite space, which contrasted with the warm sanctuary of the Clangers' world, and some of the caves within the planet held mysterious recesses lost in the gloom. For the new series, which kids might watch on their own using tablets etc., it was deemed sensible to turn up the brightness a tad. We gave the Clangers a few more caves, too. Major has a workshop of his own and Mother, with a sudden interest in horticulture, now enjoys a blooming subterranean garden. Peter produced sketches to inspire the set builders. One sketch for Mother's garden-cave included ancient ruins of fallen pillars, to suggest a long lost civilization – but this was one idea that remained on the page.

Without Oliver's "sunshine on warm Bakelite" voice, we needed someone who could engender the same gentle surrender in young souls, so it was a wonderful moment for me to hear that Michael Palin, perhaps the best-loved Englishman alive, was up for it. After accompanying us around the world, it seemed only sensible for him to pack his bags once again and keep us company in the only place he had yet to go: outer-space. William Shatner was whistled on-board to narrate the first series for the US, something quite mind-boggling to me as Captain Kirk feels like a

deity from an unreachable realm.

Then there were stories to cook up – and I was keen to contribute. I sat in my work-shed in anxious contemplation. What are the Clangers up to now? And furthermore, what do I do with a chicken made of iron, a dragon who brews soup, flying bovine, orange avocado-shaped beasts who pop out of a top hat, not to mention a cloud and a planet of brass horns? Well, luckily enough, the stories seemed to bubble up nicely. The Clangers settled into more defined characters, a family with foibles and desires of their own, rather than a general species, as in the original. "Write about what you know!" they say. So Major Clanger, the avid inventor – who was undeniably Oliver – became more so. Someone I remember forever busy, tinkering around with peculiar inventions made from whatever was around, with varying success.

And then there were the visitors who, as long as they weren't too expensive to make, could pop down to the planet for one-off adventures. If they proved popular, they could pop back again for more fun-and-games. Such beings as the Eggbots: robotic singing eggs who fitted inside each

other like Russian dolls. That episode bagged us a BAFTA.

When I first mooted the idea of bringing back *The Clangers*, Peter reacted in familiar fashion to new ideas about Smallfilms things – he was wary and "retired". However there were always two sides to Peter, and I could see a twinkle in his eye.

Once we got going, ideas about certain episodes would soon after bring forth maps, sketches, watercolours and even finished models. We went off on trips to Manchester together to catch up with what was going on, and stayed over for meals and chats.

Peter passed away in 2018, just short of his ninetieth birthday. It remains a comfort to me that I had a chance to work with him and that we had such a fun time together during his Indian summer of creativity.

The Clangers continues to be made and has proved to be a huge hit for CBeebies. And here we now are, fifty years after the original series launched and on our third series of the new *Clangers*, which will go out on CBeebies – on the anniversary of the first lunar landing. I'm still in my shed. ○

THE GREATEST SHOW

Circus250

DR DEA BIRKETT

—

Dr Dea Birkett

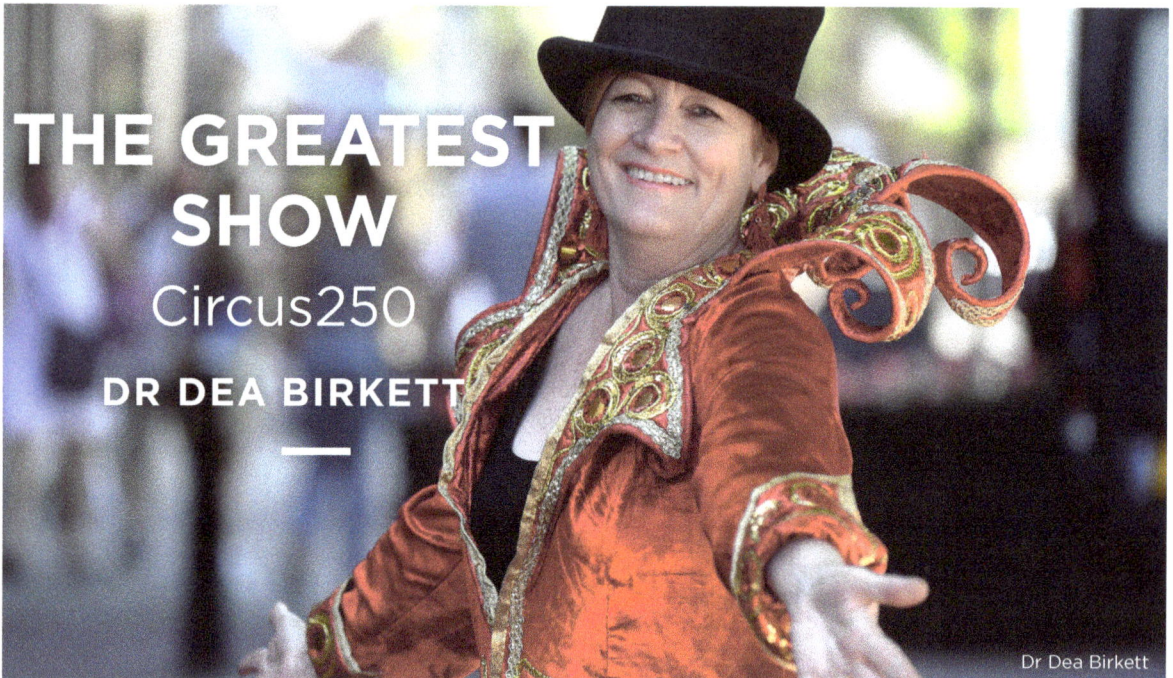

Just over 250 years ago, on an abandoned patch of marshland near London Waterloo, showman, entrepreneur and equestrian riders Philip Astley and his wife Patty laid out a 42-foot ring with a piece of rope, and filled it with astounding physical acts – jugglers, acrobats, clowns, strongmen and bareback riders.

It was 1768: a time of revolutions. But the real revolution the Astleys created was a whole new art-form; this spectacle was the world's very first circus.

Circus is Britain's most successful and enduring cultural export. 250 years after the Astleys created the first ring, circus is a worldwide phenomenon trouping around Australia, India, America and throughout the European continent. In Switzerland, Circus Knie is

as important a cultural phenomenon as our Royal Opera. French television regularly broadcasts circus-acts and the Centre National des Artes du Cirque is an established part of the French educational system. Australian acrobatic company Circa performs in London's Barbican and Hull's General Cemetery. CircusFest 2018, held at the Roundhouse, London, profiled the Palestinian Circus School and Circus Kathmandu. Circus

Aoife Raleigh and Maria Corcoran in StrongWomen Science (a Circus250 show)

54

Abyssinia appeared at the Royal Variety Performance.

Circus in Britain today is still recognisably the stuff of children's storybooks. There are tumblers, acrobats, contortionists, trapezes and clowns. There are boys in tights, girls in sequinned outfits, and fishnets still stretched over powerful thighs. The thrill is still physical, and the possibility of a fall ever-present.

But circus has had to evolve into new forms of expression, faced with the challenges of live entertainment and spiraling costs of the travelling life. In the same radical spirit in which the Astleys founded the very first performance, circus has been reworked and reinvented by contemporary companies such as the female-led, London-based Upswing and Mimbre.

My personal favourite outcome of the Circus250 year has been witnessing these changes. Traditional circuses have filled proscenium stages, such as Cirque Berserk in Sadler's Wells Peacock Theatre. Contemporary circuses have reflected on their roots

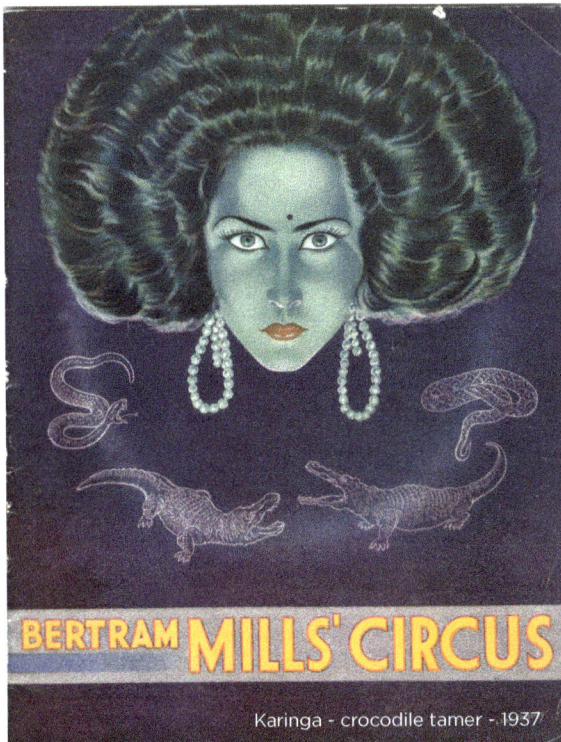

Karinga - crocodile tamer - 1937

and taken to touring in big tops and performing in a ring, such as NoFit State's new show *Lexicon*.

Circus has reached into places, and therefore audiences, which would have been unimaginable just a few years ago. This isn't without its challenges – but it is with hope.

Here's to another century of excellent circus in Britain.

John McColgan, Founder of Riverdance, Producer, Director and Circus250 Champion: "The circus came every year to Ferns in County Wexford. And every year when we saw the posters, I had to beg my mother for the sixpence to see it. Then I went and I stepped into another world entirely: a fantasy world. The astonishing women, the sweetness of the candy floss, the sawdust ring, all transported me to another place.

"In the heart of Ireland in the 1950s, it was an extraordinary, romantic experience. I was fascinated by the colour, the smell, and the life of the circus people. Their life seemed to be so exotic compared to my life in black-and-white Ireland. Every year I had the money, I went to the circus.

"I still go to the circus and I'm now bringing my granddaughter. You can see the awe and wonder in her eyes. It is still a magic world."

Sir Peter Luff, Chair, National Lottery Heritage Fund: "My love affair with circus began over 55 years ago, with my oldest friend – Gary Smart, grandson of the almost legendary Billy Smart of Billy Smart's Circus,. Gary told me great stories of circus and, green with envy, I watched him in the televised Smart's Christmas show.

"Our school took us to see the circus at Olympia each year – ironically, the great rival circus to Billy Smart's – Bertram Mills. And my love of circus was born.

"Circus can still tear young people away from TV screens and computer games, from Snapchat and Instagram. Because, however big or small, circus is fun, brash, skillful, amusing, stylish and often dangerous.

"The appeal of circus cuts across generations, age and class, thrilling and

delighting everyone who is prepared to surrender to its charms. It is a genuinely inclusive art-form. Great artists have been inspired by it. Our language and culture are illuminated by it. Circus metaphors are everywhere.

"There were Circus250 celebrations in our national museums and great art institutions. But the celebrations that matter are the ones every day in every Big Top, every stage, every venue where circus is performed, in communities the length and breadth of the land. In each of these performances, circus brings terror, delight, pleasure, laughter, spectacular thrills and smiles to thousands of children of all ages."

Jack Jay, Producer and Director, Great Yarmouth Hippodrome: "Nothing embodies the celebrations of Circus250 quite like The Hippodrome, Great Yarmouth, where the historic atmosphere captures your imagination as soon as you enter. Built in 1903 by legendary showman George Gilbert, it's Britain's last remaining total circus-building. The mechanical water-ring transforms into a gigantic pool; an original feature, restored in 1979 by my father Peter Jay. It's been in use every season since.

"The Hippodrome has been proudly owned by my family for almost 40 years. During my father's years as Producer and Director of our shows, he endeavoured to drive the art-form forward, committed to finding a place for circus in the modern entertainment world. He drew upon his experience as a 1960s pop star by using modern music and exciting concert-style lighting, and bringing the audience right into the show. He called it "circus for the MTV generation". Although frowned upon at the time, it became the blueprint for many circuses across Europe for decades to come.

"Now, as Producer and Director of our shows myself, I'm striving for the same innovation. We produce four brand-new shows each year – some of them a theatre-

Lost in Translation Circus - photo by Pete Maclaine, courtesy of Circus250

circus hybrid, including actors and immersive theatrical-sets. In our award-winning *Pirates Live!* show, a 50-foot galleon dominates a movie-style set, based around our water-spectacle. But at the show's heart remains the world-class, jaw-dropping circus performers.

"The Hippodrome doesn't stand as a window into the past or a relic of a bygone age. We embrace our history and use it to push our shows forward – and further into the future."

What next? CIRCUS250 in 2019

With such enormous media attention, the profile of circus in the UK has risen. Circus250, a community interest company that coordinates the anniversary celebration, has created three new shows. *StrongWomen Science*, *The Secret Life of a Circus Caravan* and *Meet My Circus Family* are all touring in 2019, under the Circus250 banner. The *Women in Circus* film is available for screening at events, conferences and exhibitions.

As we say in the circus, we hope to see you "on the road". ◯

For bookings, contact: ringmaster@circus250.org

To order a copy of the Circus250 Souvenir Book, email: bigtop@circus250.org

Find out more about Circus250 at: www.circus250.org

logo designed by Sir Peter Blake

POWERFUL PREFERENCES
Highlights from Ofcom's Making Sense of Media research

Media literacy affords people the skills, knowledge and understanding to make full use of the opportunities presented by both traditional and new communications services. Ofcom has a duty to promote and research media literacy, and we carry out a range of studies to better understand this area. We call this research: *Making Sense of Media*.

One of our key pieces of research is our annual quantitative *Children and Parents' Media Use and Attitudes Tracker*, which provides detailed evidence on media access, use and understanding among children aged three to fifteen (and their parents).

This infographic (on the right) provides a snapshot of how children of different ages use and interact with different types of media.

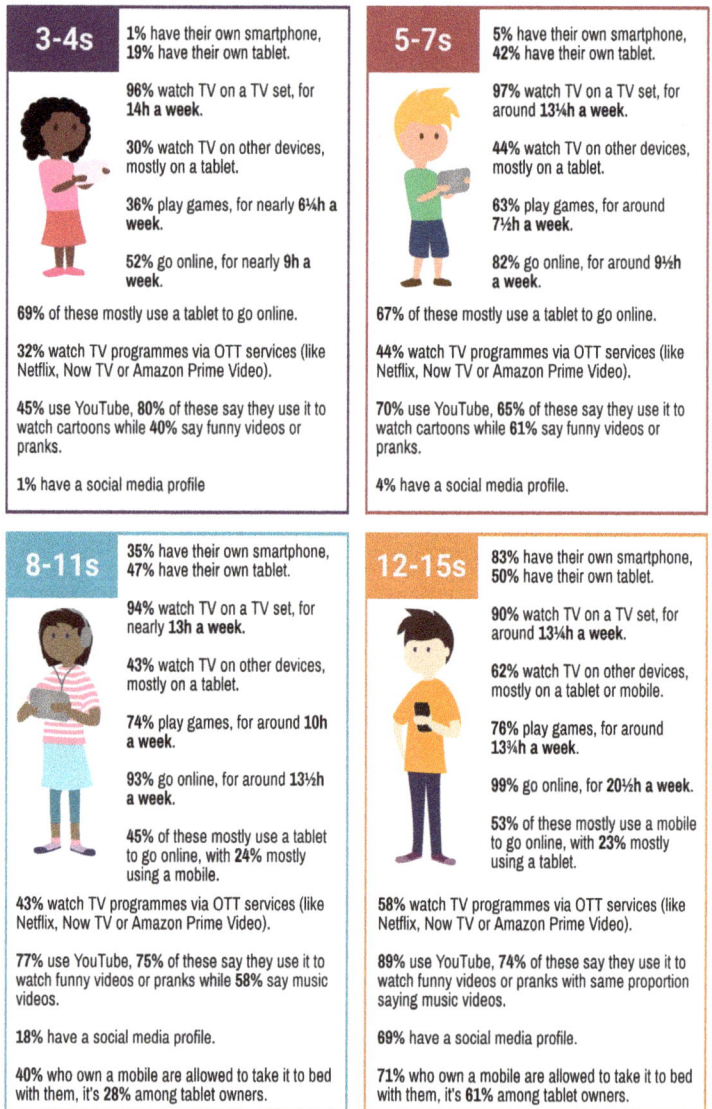

3-4s

1% have their own smartphone, 19% have their own tablet.

96% watch TV on a TV set, for 14h a week.

30% watch TV on other devices, mostly on a tablet.

36% play games, for nearly 6¼h a week.

52% go online, for nearly 9h a week.

69% of these mostly use a tablet to go online.

32% watch TV programmes via OTT services (like Netflix, Now TV or Amazon Prime Video).

45% use YouTube, 80% of these say they use it to watch cartoons while 40% say funny videos or pranks.

1% have a social media profile

5-7s

5% have their own smartphone, 42% have their own tablet.

97% watch TV on a TV set, for around 13¼h a week.

44% watch TV on other devices, mostly on a tablet.

63% play games, for around 7½h a week.

82% go online, for around 9½h a week.

67% of these mostly use a tablet to go online.

44% watch TV programmes via OTT services (like Netflix, Now TV or Amazon Prime Video).

70% use YouTube, 65% of these say they use it to watch cartoons while 61% say funny videos or pranks.

4% have a social media profile.

8-11s

35% have their own smartphone, 47% have their own tablet.

94% watch TV on a TV set, for nearly 13h a week.

43% watch TV on other devices, mostly on a tablet.

74% play games, for around 10h a week.

93% go online, for around 13½h a week.

45% of these mostly use a tablet to go online, with 24% mostly using a mobile.

43% watch TV programmes via OTT services (like Netflix, Now TV or Amazon Prime Video).

77% use YouTube, 75% of these say they use it to watch funny videos or pranks while 58% say music videos.

18% have a social media profile.

40% who own a mobile are allowed to take it to bed with them, it's 28% among tablet owners.

12-15s

83% have their own smartphone, 50% have their own tablet.

90% watch TV on a TV set, for around 13¼h a week.

62% watch TV on other devices, mostly on a tablet or mobile.

76% play games, for around 13¾h a week.

99% go online, for 20½h a week.

53% of these mostly use a mobile to go online, with 23% mostly using a tablet.

58% watch TV programmes via OTT services (like Netflix, Now TV or Amazon Prime Video).

89% use YouTube, 74% of these say they use it to watch funny videos or pranks with same proportion saying music videos.

69% have a social media profile.

71% who own a mobile are allowed to take it to bed with them, it's 61% among tablet owners.

Key findings from the 2018 research:

- TV sets and tablets dominate device use, but time spent watching TV on a TV set (broadcast or on demand) is decreasing.

- Children in the UK (aged five to fifteen) spend around 20 minutes more online, in a typical day, than they do in front of a TV set.

- Children's time online is estimated at an average of 2 hours 11 minutes per day – while their average daily TV time has fallen year-on-year by almost 8 minutes, to an estimated 1 hour 52 minutes.

- The viewing landscape is complex, with half of five to fifteen year olds watching OTT television services like Netflix, Amazon Prime Video and Now TV.

- YouTube is becoming the viewing platform of choice used by 80% of children, with rising popularity particularly among eight to eleven year olds.

- Among those who watch both YouTube and TV programmes on a TV set, nearly half of "tweens" aged eight to eleven and older children aged twelve to fifteen (49%) prefer watching content on YouTube. However, more than a third get the same enjoyment from both viewing experiences.

Aged 8-11  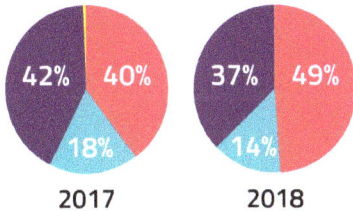   **Aged 12-15**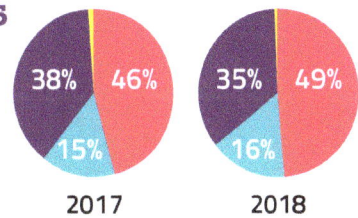

● Prefer to watch YouTube video   ● Prefer to watch programmes on a TV set   ● Like both the same   ● Don't know/not sure

- Online gaming is increasingly popular; three-quarters of five to fifteen year olds who play games do so online.

- A majority (69%) of twelve to fifteen year olds who visit websites/ apps they have not used before think critically about the sites they visit, and whether they trust the information on them to be true or accurate. But only a third correctly understand search engine advertising.

- Children are being exposed to unwanted experiences online; 16% of eight to eleven year olds and 31% of twelve to fifteen year olds who go online have seen something online that they found worrying or nasty. However, almost all recall being taught how to use the internet safely.

- There has been an increase in parents of twelve to fifteen year olds – and of twelve to fifteen year olds themselves – saying that controlling screen time has become harder. However, most twelve to fifteen year olds (63%) believe they have a struck a good balance between screen time and doing other things.

Life on the small screen: what children are watching and why

To help understand *why* children are drawn towards online content, in autumn 2018 Ofcom undertook a detailed qualitative study of children's viewing.

We interviewed 40 children from across the UK, aged four to sixteen. Data collection was a three-stage process: children were asked to complete a seven-day media diary; we collected passive data of device use and online media history; and, finally, we conducted three-hour in-home interviews with the children, plus a 15-minute interview with their parents.

The study revealed powerful preferences for choice, control and a sense of community. It found that:

- **YouTube dominates, followed by Netflix.** Children in the study overwhelmingly preferred watching YouTube (almost all children watched it daily) and Netflix, to any other platforms.

- **Live TV is parent-led and often reserved for family time.** Most of the children in the study watched live, scheduled TV, though only a small number did so daily. Live TV viewing was often convened by parents, allowing the family to come together in the main living room to watch soaps, films, quizzes or "appointment viewing" such as *Strictly Come Dancing* or *The X-Factor*. Some children used live TV to fill time, often while they were doing something else – such as eating dinner. Linear TV players were seen as useful for catch up services rather than providing on-demand services.

- **Choice and control.** Children said they valued YouTube and Netflix for offering instant control over what they were watching, and access to seemingly endless, personalised content. They rarely searched actively for content, but rather followed their subscriptions or recommended videos. Some children preferred to watch YouTube and Netflix content on their own – and mostly on their smartphone, which they felt to be more private. Many children preferred shorter content (typically less than 10 minutes) or watched parts of longer programmes; they viewed this content in snippets of time (e.g. getting ready, before dinner) rather than watching longer content in one sitting.

- **Children turn to YouTube for three things.** The study found most of the children's viewing on YouTube fell into three broad categories:

  - **Hobbies and passions.** Lots of children watched videos related to their offline interests, such as tutorials to further their passion for music or football. Some experienced similar gratification watching others participating in hands-on activities, such as arts and craft, or playing sport – to the extent that some said they no longer took part in these activities themselves in the "real world".

  - **Vloggers and community.** Many children watched vloggers or YouTubers, often connecting with them through shared passions such as sports or crafts – and enjoying becoming part of their follower communities. Lots of the children said they looked up to their favourite vloggers as role models, or regarded them as friends who could provide support or advice. This type of content also appealed to children's natural curiosity about other people's "normal" lives; they felt such videos had authenticity, which made them easy to relate to.

  - **Sensory videos.** Many children enjoyed videos which included "satisfying" noises, such as other people making and playing with slime, or opening presents. These videos are described as "Autonomous Sensory Meridian Response", due to their ability to generate a feeling of wellbeing and relaxation among some people.

Alongside the popularity of these platforms, we found children weren't spending a lot of time meeting their friends face-to-face, playing outdoors or physically pursuing hobbies or interests. Apart from organised activities, the children were spending an increasing amount of time alone in their rooms after school.

Indeed, content viewing is increasingly individualistic; whichever platform was being used, children seem most attracted to content that they can view on their own device, over which they can exercise maximum choice – and which directly feeds the things that interest them. ⊙

More information on both of the studies above and our other media literacy research can be found on our website: www.ofcom.org.uk/research-and-data/media-literacy-research

MAGIC AND MONSTERS
The FAANGs sink their teeth into children's content

RICHARD COOPER

—

US technology giants Facebook, Amazon, Apple, Netflix and Google (the FAANGs) have all now thrown their hats into the online video-streaming ring. A decade in, Netflix and Amazon Prime video could be regarded as the incumbent Video on Demand (VoD) providers; however, Facebook Watch, Apple TV and Google's YouTube Premium have now joined them in the market. In an increasingly competitive VoD sector, each of these providers is looking to use their deep pockets to secure the TV shows needed to draw consumers to their services. Children's content plays no small part in creating that compelling offer.

However, not all VoD services are created equal when it comes to the younger viewer. Facebook Watch limits access to users over the age of thirteen and, as a result, none of its commissioned shows are directed at children. Similarly YouTube Premium, which provides users with advertising-free streaming of all YouTube hosted videos, has recognised that a sizable proportion of its free content is child friendly. Subsequently, with just four exceptions, the service's commissions are all directed at older viewers. As a result, when the subject of the FAANGs is raised in the context of children's content, the focus must be on Apple, Amazon and Netflix.

Children and Family titles account for a consistent 12–13% of the catalogues of the incumbent VoD services, Amazon and Netflix, but among these services' original titles, the picture is a little different. Netflix currently has the largest catalogue of original children's content with 82 existing shows and a further 25 original titles in production. This genre of content makes up the second-largest share of Netflix's original catalogue, accounting for 20%

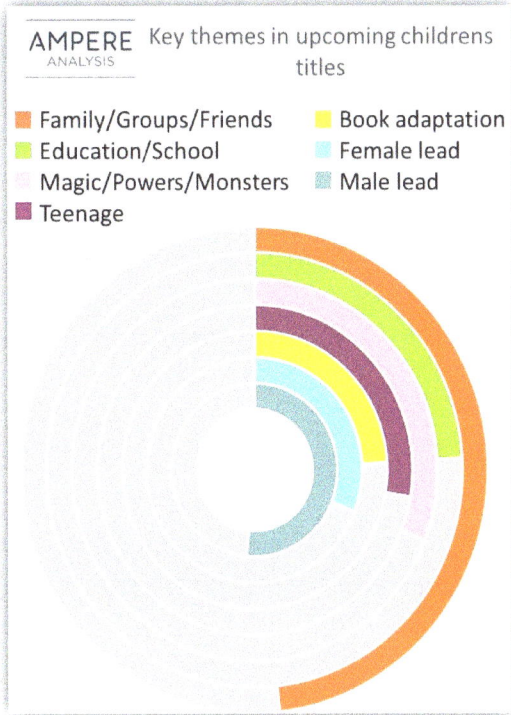

AMPERE ANALYSIS — Key themes in upcoming childrens titles

Legend:
- Family/Groups/Friends
- Education/School
- Magic/Powers/Monsters
- Teenage
- Book adaptation
- Female lead
- Male lead

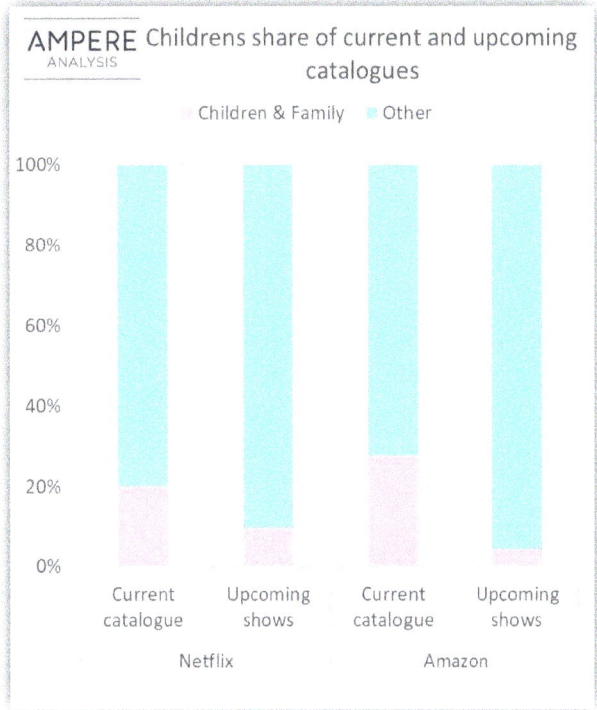

AMPERE ANALYSIS — Childrens share of current and upcoming catalogues

Children & Family / Other

Netflix: Current catalogue, Upcoming shows
Amazon: Current catalogue, Upcoming shows

– behind only Comedy, at 22%.

However, among upcoming shows, Children's accounts for only 9% of Netflix's total commissions. Amazon's original children's catalogue consists of twenty shows, but the service has just four in development; six times fewer than Netflix. Children's content accounts for 28% of Amazon's originals, the largest share of any genre, but only 4% of its new commissions.

Ampere's title-tracking shows no indication that Children and Family programming is becoming less of a focus for those services. The shortfall in original children's production is more likely indicative of a lack of success for these own-brand children's titles, and an increasing reliance on acquired content to maintain balance within their respective catalogues.

With this increased focus on acquired over original children's content, analysis of the shows still being commissioned by these players may give an indication of the types of content they need. Predictably, **animation** is the most commissioned type of children's show for both Amazon and Netflix, accounting for two thirds of all such titles. The comparative ease with which animated shows may be dubbed into other languages also reflects these services international ambitions. The incumbents are also commissioning a greater proportion of **children's sci-fi and fantasy** titles – a key genre for these services, overall. These titles make up just 3% of Netflix's current catalogue of original children's shows and 12% of Amazon's catalogue, but 12% and 25% of commissioned works respectively. Common themes within these upcoming shows are **magic, monsters and superpowers**; a third of upcoming shows commissioned by Netflix and Amazon are centred around these themes.

Shows commissioned by Amazon and Netflix often focus on a **group of characters**, or have **teenagers** as the primary character or characters. Half of shows in production for Amazon and Netflix focus on a group of friends or on a family; a quarter follow a teenager or group of teenagers. Additionally, 24% of shows in production across both companies are based on books, presumably with the hope that the familiarity of those titles will work in their favour.

Apple is the last of the FAANGs commissioning new original programming. Apple TV+, announced in March 2019, had commissioned 34 shows at the time of writing, for what is largely a VoD content aggregation platform rather than a standalone service. Apple has commissioned just two children's shows, rendering analysis at this stage somewhat moot. The titles so far are an untitled *Peanuts* animated series, and *Helpsters*, which follows the well-known Sesame Street characters as they educate children on different topics (including how to code!). The latter certainly is in line with the tech giant's stated aim of providing educational programming to support the service's family focus.

Outside of children's content, Apple's other commissions echo the genre spread of Netflix, and to a lesser degree Amazon; an indication of the platform's intended broader appeal and one that will no doubt be reflected in its children's content acquisition.

All the FAANGs will need to bolster their services against the launch of Disney+, scheduled for Q3 2019 in the US and globally through 2020. Disney's family-friendly branding will force greater competition for family viewing and push those VoD players competing in that space to secure the strongest non-Disney children's titles. Netflix's licensing of the Roald Dahl's story rights in late 2018 is indicative of these moves.

In addition, the streamers will also need to supplement their children's catalogues with new titles – and with their failure to create compelling originals in the genre, this will necessitate acquiring such works. ◯

LIVING IN AN ECHO CHAMBER

The relationship between young people and music

SARAH DE CAUX

In this digital age, music remains hugely important and emotive for young people. It helps them live their lives positively, and their relationship with music has been heightened and intensified by their often limitless access to it through technology. It continues to have a huge influence on how young people forge their identity and navigate critical points in their lives.

However, while this relationship remains fundamental, it is also in flux. Join the Dots' research, sponsored by PRS, highlights how these changes are manifesting themselves as well as some of their implications for content creators.

Technology is changing the way young people attend to music

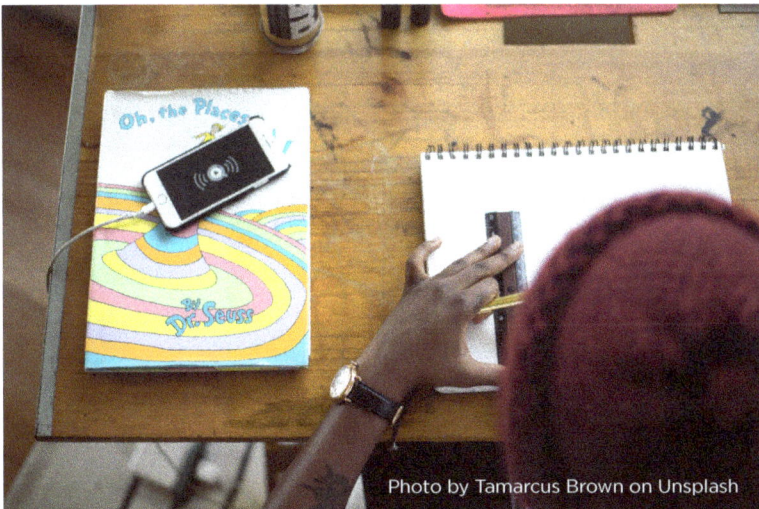

Photo by Tamarcus Brown on Unsplash

Thanks to technology, music is ubiquitous; young people can listen to it from sun up to sun down. But despite the fact that it's always there (which has been facilitated by technology like smartphones and platforms like the streaming services), young people often give their music very little focused or critical attention.

Alongside this, with technology providing direct and immediate access to cultural content from vloggers, YouTubers and gamers, music is now vying for attention against a maelstrom of often free to consume content on any topic of interest.

With limitless access to music, young people often do not carefully consider where music comes from, how it is made, or whether/how artists are paid. And if that's happening with music, it's likely happening with other forms of content too. Boundaries between "official" and "unofficial" are blurring for many – and young people don't necessarily understand or care about the differences, whatever content creators may think…

Young people are living in a music echo chamber

Photo by Siddharth Bhogra on Unsplash

In our research, young people were embracing the algorithms streaming services use to tailor content for them, picking up what the platform recommends and enjoying that it feels "personal" to them. As a result, this is a generation for whom music discovery has become a frequently passive process. There is little sign that they are questioning or challenging the motivations driving these algorithms, or that they are applying a critical mindset here.

But while much of their discovery is in the digital space, young people are "ambidextrous"; they can fluidly switch between digital and non-digital platforms to find new music and interact.

Digital sharing of music is important, but we observed the assertion of agency and private (versus public) boundaries. Young

people often preferred not to share music publicly. Instead, they would only do so with a select group of trusted friends via face-to-face and "dark social" channels (such as WhatsApp groups).

This is because sharing music is, for younger audiences, an intimate act: one that can strengthen social bonds, but that can equally make one vulnerable and open to ridicule.

The model of influence has changed

The advent of digital platforms has changed the way music is disseminated and how influence spreads. The dissemination process used to be linear, spreading from the creator through the connector to the consumer. Now, influence is shared.

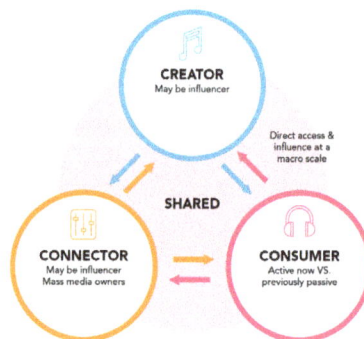

Image copyright: Join the Dots (Research) Ltd

Social media platforms have connected creators directly to audiences, removing the need for an intermediary and shifting the dynamics of influence. Intermediaries still play a role in

introducing consumers to creators – especially when the creator is more obscure and seeks exposure – although these connectors tend to be individual "supersharers", rather than the more traditional corporate channels.

But in a nutshell, this generation see that social media is connecting them directly (at least in theory) to their idols. They seek out and are coming to expect this connection. It's a fundamental way in which they are engaging with and discovering new music content.

Conclusion

In our study with PRS for Music, the young people to whom we spoke had a dichotomous relationship with music: ubiquitous, but competing with a free mindset. They cherished rather than challenged – or questioned – the algorithms feeding them content and loved to share, albeit often privately (particularly for younger teens).

Ultimately, they are "Generation YouTube". It's part of the fabric of their world, but they are masters at weaving seamlessly between the offline and digital environments. And however it is found or consumed, music remains a hugely emotive topic for young people today.

Photo by Sharon McCutcheon from Pexels

STONES IN THEIR POCKETS
How children play & designing for children

ALISON NORRINGTON

—

Ever bought a child an exciting gift in a glossy box, only to find that they're more engaged with making a "spaceship" from the box than playing with the gift – which now lies discarded to the side?

The CMC's "Stones in their Pockets" looks at the fundamentals of play and how kids interact with objects in different ways than we, as adults, expect; but also how a child's imagination is fuelled and influenced by natural materials in their environment. "Stones in their Pockets" frames a key question around learning through play, kids' imaginations and discoverability: if we're overloading kids with content and information, and giving away too many answers, are we depriving them of the opportunity to discover and come to their own conclusions – and so, nurture their imaginations?

"Stones in their Pockets" is inspired by Paula Rautio's 2013 article entitled "Children who Carry Stones in their Pockets",[1] which was introduced by Dylan Yamada-Rice during a roadshow event on VR+Kids research that storycentral conducted for Children's Media Foundation in 2018 – which came to a finale at the Royal College of Art in January 2019. The research roadshow bought together storytellers, experienced designers, academics and content-creators, and was hosted by Dubit in Leeds, by The Immersive Storytelling Studio at National Theatre in London and by Immotion in Manchester, with a core focus on our

---

1   For more information, visit: commonworlds.net/childrens-relations-with-materials/
children-who-carry-stones-in-their-pockets/

responsibility to children during their most responsive and susceptible years of growth.

At the Manchester event, hosted by Immotion, conversation arose around how children play – and how, as storytellers and experienced designers, we can work with that natural behaviour flow rather than try to guide it too heavily. Dylan Yamada-Rice of Dubit and RCA introduced the group to the work of Rautio by telling an anecdote about a parent who found their six year old son returning home from school every day with, literally, stones in his trouser pockets. Every evening the mother would tip out the dusty stones, only to find more in his pockets the next evening. This happened for a few days until, exasperated at having to collect new stones every day, the boy told his Mum to "please stop throwing away my Star Wars galaxy rocks!"

It emerged how not having access to popular culture toys in schools meant children were using found objects from the playground (in this case, stones and bits of tarmac) to become improvised and important parts of a self-created Star Wars game. As a group we were intrigued and fascinated; the story quickly led to a series of personal recounts of experiences with our own children, or as kids ourselves.

CMC's "Stones in their Pockets" speaker Carol Chell was *PlaySchool* presenter from 1966–88, and writer and Head of Preschool Programming for The Children's Channel until 1998. Carol demonstrates how she would try to make something, often from cardboard loo-roll holders, PVA glue and crumpled tissue-paper – giving the children the freedom to

be creative in their own way, rather than struggle to follow a precise approach.

"Stones in their Pockets" introduces the essence of play through developmental stages, play patterns, age transitions and the daily lives of kids, from the important perspective of how storytellers, toy-makers, technology providers and anybody designing content or experiences for children can mindfully design for kids rather than adults.

The fact is that play and design have a lot in common – it is imaginative, creative, explorative, iterative, meaningful, emotional and engaging. To reach a "play-state" you have to go through the design process with an open mind, let yourself be surprised and embrace unexpected opportunities. This requires a safe and trustful environment – as play does – and an understanding of the process as an essential journey for meaningful design. Designers and content creators sometimes lack access to children or their worlds when creating products, images, experiences and environments for them. Therefore, fine distinctions between age transitions and the day-to-day experiences of children are often overlooked.

Picasso once said, on playfulness, that he had "spent a lifetime trying to paint like a child"; the "Stones in their Pockets" concept, along with some of the best practices defined by the storycentral VR+Kids research for Children's Media Foundation, explores the ingredients to consider when inventing something new and how to reach a "play-state". ◯

STREAM IF YOU WANNA GO FASTER

A Golden Age of kids' programming?

RACHEL MURRELL

—

We're often told this is a Golden Age of television. The arrival of Netflix, Amazon, YouTube TV and so on has brought new outlets, new money and new shows. And that's got to be good, right?

Well, it is if you're a viewer of what we used to call "Primetime Drama", with cracking shows like *The Crown*, *The Handmaid's Tale*, *Stranger Things*, *Transparent* and *Sex Education* garnering attention and awards. And that surely creates opportunities for the companies making such shows.

But is the same true in the kids' space? Are the new platforms offering anything like the same amount of new content for Under 16s?

At first look, it seems they are: according to Tim Westcott of IHS Markit, Netflix made 143 hours of original children's programming in 2018, and Amazon 45 hours. In fact, that's a significant fall for Netflix – down from 241 hours in 2017 – but it's still considerable. And, according to Ofcom's Media Nation report of 2018, investment in new UK children's programming by public service broadcasters, already falling, has declined by a further 18% in real terms in 2017 to £70 million.

With Disney+ and AppleTV+ coming on stream this autumn, and new services from NBCUniversal, DHX and TimeWarner, there will be new platforms and more opportunities for kids' programming than ever before. There will also be new holes opening up on Netflix where the Disney content used to be.

In short, the competition for good shows is about to increase.

Netflix is moving into a new phase. Having been a mass acquirer of kids' content, it began to commission it five years ago – under Andy Yeatman, its original kids' slate grew in three years from two titles to 40 – and is now starting to become an owner. In May this year, it bought the multi award-winning *StoryBots* brand from creators Evan and Gregg Spiridellis. There have been rumours of a kids' production hub.

The move into creating its own kids' brands – doubtless accelerated by the impending arrival of Disney+ – is a way to secure exclusive content, and avoid the kinds of spiraling production costs and talent price-wars that platforms hate. It also creates consumer goods potential and, by snagging a high-profile educational brand, it sends a signal to aspirational parents that it is the home of quality kids' content.

But you don't have to be *StoryBots* to get a Netflix commission – as UK producers from Lime Television to Darrall Macqueen can testify.

The risk for producers is that, in such an ocean of content, it's hard to make your show stand out. And if viewers can't find it, the algorithms won't work in your favour.

Another risk is that new commissions are chosen to attract global audiences and so shows with a strong national or regional sensibility either don't get commissioned,

or disappear when they do. Whereas public broadcasters such as CBBC have done much to diversify talent on, and behind, the screen, it's hard to see the global streamers continuing this good work.

But it's not impossible. By 2017, Netflix was acquiring kids and family content from more than 50 countries, and commissioning it in ten. While most will come from the US, followed by Canada, the UK and Australia, Netflix has deep pockets and limitless (see what I did there?) space, allowing the company to commission from other countries too. And the long-tail effect is that shows can claim success if they accrue large audiences over time, rather than having to do so at launch.

According to Ofcom's *Children and Parents: Media Use and Attitudes Report 2018*, published in January, TV sets and tablets dominate device use, but time spent watching TV on a TV set (broadcast or on demand) is decreasing. The number of children watching Netflix, Amazon Prime Video and Now TV grows from 32% of three to four year olds to 58% of twelve to fifteen year olds.

But the SVoDs aren't having it all their own way. Ofcom reports that YouTube is becoming the viewing platform of choice for children. Some 45% of three to four year olds watch it, particularly for animations. This rises to 89% among twelve to fifteen year olds, with a strong preference for pranks and humour, and some music. And when not watching YouTube, kids are playing digital games. For 36% of three to five year olds, this takes up over six hours a week – rising to nearly 14 hours a week for

76% of twelve to fifteen year olds.

Small wonder, then, that Netflix and the others are making a determined effort to woo kids with original content: interactive shows such as *Battle Kitty* and *Minecraft: Story Mode*.

We don't know what's coming, but projections by IHS Markit suggest that Disney+ may have 20 million households in the US by 2023, against Netflix' 70 million and Amazon's 30 million. Some of those households will have kids, but by no means all.

The battle is on – not just to attract new subscribers, but to keep them. And for the SVoDs, that means providing something for *everyone* in the household. The streamers want to offer great kids' content, not out of a social commitment, but because without it they have less traction in households with children. Kids reduce audience churn, and that's good for business.

Now they're all trying to find the signature programming that will allow them to do that. ⟡

Reference:
Ofcom (2019): *Children and Parents: Media Use and Attitudes Report 2018*

Photo by Marc Schäfer on Unsplash

A REASON TO BE CHEERFUL – PART 1

The £57 million Young Audiences Content Fund

JACKIE EDWARDS

—

It's a funny old world, although there doesn't seem to be a lot to laugh about currently. Leaving all the global, European and British political brow-furrowing items aside, and looking just at our own British kids media industry doorstep – we've not had a lot to be optimistic about.

The last decade has seen a cavalcade of business challenges: advertising restrictions, changes in audience consumption habits and the rise and rise and *rise* of the FAANGs. This has all led to a complicated, confusing picture. SVOD and AVOD platforms dominate the UK landscape, in production finance opportunity, shoutiness and, seemingly, audience appreciation.

Meanwhile, the last decade has seen a steep decline in the provision of public service programming for children and young people.

Does that matter, I hear you ask?

Depends on the level of importance you place on public service content – how it can support and enrich early childhood, explain and broaden children's knowledge and their understanding of the world, entertainingly explain and reassure the chaos of teen years … and all of this not only subscription free, but carefully curated in a safe environment.

It informs, it educates and it entertains. It's the stuff that speaks specifically to our young people, and helps shape and define our cultural identity. I'd say it matters.

Times have been tough for public service content, but thanks to a huge amount of dedicated lobbying, a clear analysis of the decline of kids' public service content by Ofcom and, moreover, a stellar decision by the UK Government, a glimmer of hope has emerged for this sector. The government have given UK audiences a splendid gift in the form of the £57 million Young Audiences Content Fund (YACF), a three year pilot administered by the BFI.

The YACF is a very big reason to be cheerful. I say Part 1, because this is a Pilot – and while we need to start thinking about what Part 2 might look like, our collective endeavour should be to make Part 1 as successful as it possibly can be.

This is an amazing opportunity and it shouldn't be wasted. It's for all of us, producers, broadcasters, distributors to make this work so audiences will continue to have access to an array of brilliant public service content.

As a creative community, we ALL need to engage with the Fund as fully as we can. Whether you're applying for development or production support, thinking of commissioning a couple of additional shows or can mentor young talent with big potential – if you have an idea to make the Fund work better, or just want to shout about the wonders of the Fund in the street, please do. All of it. We need everyone's active participation, opinions, celebration, communication.

What we show this country's young people really matters; let's ensure that we continue the UK's heritage of making brilliant, culturally defining, enduring programmes for our most important audiences.

The YACF Pilot is a game changer – a reason to be cheerful. Help make sure there is a YACF Part 2! Get engaged with the Fund:

www.bfi.org.uk/supporting-uk-film/production-development-funding/young-audiences-content-fund ◯

TACKLING TEENS
The new generation of trans people

FOX FISHER

—

People often look to the media to form their opinions. The medium of film has the power to reach audiences that print media may not be able to access, portraying messages in a creative, visual and emotive way. This is particularly true when it comes down to shaping people's attitudes towards underrepresented groups. We've all seen a film or a series that completely transformed our thoughts on a particular issue.

Seven long years ago, I was a part of a mainstream documentary called *My Transsexual Summer*. The show was the first mainstream documentary about transgender issues in the UK, and opened up a dialogue with the nation. Despite the show being transformative and pioneering for it's time – because, for many, it was the first time they ever got an insight into the lives of trans people – it didn't necessarily portray trans issues in a realistic and an authentic way.

I was unable to truly describe my experience of my gender as a non-binary trans person and I felt betrayed by the makers of the documentary. It was explained to me that my gender identity was "too complicated" for the audience to understand.

This is why I picked up a camera myself and started filming the people around me. That's how My Genderation came to be, a film project that was started by myself and Lewis Hancox – a co-star on the show. Seven years on, My Genderation has over a hundred short films on trans issues, some which have been shown on the BBC (*New Genderation*) and C4 (*My Trans Story*). Our films are also shown at film festivals all around the world, and used to educate and celebrate trans lives. We've made work for the NHS, Stonewall campaigns, Transgender Europe, PrEP and more.

At My Genderation, we are having our own transition from short format to longer format. We are also starting to create more fiction. The reason why our films are unique is because they are created entirely by trans people, about trans people, for everyone. Naturally, this makes our focus and portrayal of trans issues more authentic, engaging and real.

We don't fall into the trap of sensationalism, or focus solely on trans people's bodies or surgeries. We elevate the voices of so many more within our communities, and not just the tired trope of the white older trans woman.

One of the most important voices we elevate, is that of young people: the new generation of trans people. Research shows that young trans kids are suffering, with over 84% of trans pupils having self harmed and 45% having attempted suicide (Stonewall School Report, 2017). This is primarily due to the bullying and stigma that they face, and the lack of access to services and social support they require.

These numbers are so much lower for kids who get the social support they need. Trans people are able to come out at a much younger age, due to more open discussions about these issues. Years of isolation, shame and the "wrong puberty" can be prevented, and we can protect the mental health of our young people by allowing them to be themselves.

And no, this doesn't mean surgeries on children. It means allowing the kids to express their gender the way they want, supporting them through a social transition and give them access to puberty blockers once they hit puberty (if that's what they need). Puberty blockers allow them time to breathe and figure out who they are, and

have no permanent or irreversible effects. It's simply a pause on puberty. When young trans people are allowed to come into their own, it can ease gender dysphoria and fight depression, and so allow these individuals a much brighter future.

This is why it's so heartening to see representation of trans issues in content for young audiences. This includes shows such as CBBC's *I Am Leo* (BAFTA nominated) and *Just A Girl* (hated by the *Daily Mail*). This type of content allows young audiences to learn about the experiences of peers who might be different from them, and helps foster understanding and reduce bullying.

This is one of the main reasons my partner and I created *The Trans Teen Survival Guide*. We wanted the book we wish we'd had growing up: a go-to book that could not only answer all the questions we had, but would also be a valuable resource to show how to support a trans person. Most importantly, we wanted trans kids to see themselves represented in young adult literature.

Since its release less than a year ago, this book has been a great success and is being well received within our community and beyond. It's clear that there is a need for content of this kind; we need more representation of the new face of trans. Not only is it important that trans kids and trans people can see themselves represented, but it helps others understand and empathise with our struggles. It is so much easier to reach people's hearts and minds when our experiences are humanised, and we aren't just the "scary trans people" the media bang on about.

The Trans Teen Survival Guide offers valuable insight into the lives of trans teens, focusing on a variety of challenges, issues and valuable information about the trans community. It also offers people's experiences, with many people's stories and thoughts about things like coming out, how to choose a new name, how to use a binder more safely, how to deal with dysphoria, awkward yet funny situations trans people find themselves in and much, much more.

These types of resources need to be adapted into different forms of media in order to reach more people. *The Trans Teen Survival Guide* is a perfect example of a message that can be adapted into not just books, but art and film. The trans community is full of informative, fun and engaging content. All creators need to do is take a chance on us.

And remember: nothing about us, without us! ⊙

Press Release for *The Trans Teen Survival Guide*:
docs.google.com/document/d/14UTuVG1eATH1AtXKdWEd6e9BipO2uI2So9MSvUr_eB0/edit
My Genderation: www.mygenderation.com

Owl and Fox Fisher

Alex Collier

WRITERS ASSEMBLE!

EMMA REEVES

—

Media never stands still, but the employment prospects for TV writers are changing hugely at the moment. The superstar status of big US showrunners and the packaging row which is currently engulfing the Writers' Guild of America, agents and writers, may seem a very long way away from the world of children's media in the UK. But it's a timely reminder of the power that writers have as the original creators, without which there would be no shows.

The ever-growing power of the SVODs has shaken the "traditional" broadcasters, who are growing increasingly concerned about the competition for talent from on-demand platforms. There's a big appetite for content, but, aside from Continuing Drama (soap), we're seeing a move towards shorter and more "authored" series, which are more often led by writer-showrunners instead of non-writing producers.

For TV writers, this has both advantages and drawbacks. For those with showrunning aspirations, there's a slightly better chance of achieving those ambitions – however, the British system has not historically provided many on-the-job training opportunities for writer-showrunners. So we're seeing European companies looking to America for experienced showrunners, who can end up overworked as they try to run several shows at once! For jobbing writers, there are also fewer "story of the week" shows providing chances to showcase your own voice whilst developing your craft, contacts and CV.

Most awkwardly, writers are put in the delicate position of having to hire and fire each other. With the insatiable demand for returnable series, there are "reluctant showrunners" who would prefer to write all the episodes themselves but are compelled by pressures of time or orders from above to hire other writers, some of whom may end up feeling they were set up to fail. (The Writers' Guild of Great Britain is in the process of creating guidelines for writer-showrunners and those who work with them.)

In children's television, we are all very used to working with lead writers – although the level of autonomy and control of the overall vision afforded to that lead writer varies enormously. I have worked as a children's television writer for over fifteen years now, and have written on shows in a wide range of genres: animation, live action, gritty realistic drama, sitcom, mystery, musical comedy, action-adventure, science fiction and fantasy. I have been the lead writer, worked with other lead writers and I have also worked on shows with no lead writer. I would *always* rather follow the guidance of another lead writer than work on a show without one

– or on one of those unhappy shows where a lead writer is undermined or ignored by producers.

A successful show needs a strong authorial vision and over the years I have worked with many brilliant people who have provided that unique spark. They are, all too often, wonderfully creative but far too humble and modest – and, as a result, minimally credited and criminally underpaid.

For too long, this has been true of "children's television" as a whole. But although traditional children's programming is always under threat, additional platforms are opening up new worlds of opportunity for programme-making aimed at, and centred around, young people – who can now decide exactly what they want to watch and when they want to watch it.

We writers need to be ready to exploit those opportunities. How long have we all been bemoaning the fact that we'd love to write about a certain subject matter, in a particular tone, but unfortunately there are only one or two channels who are prepared to make shows which are led and driven by young characters? And that it would never pass their editorial guidelines without being watered down past recognition?

Although it can be challenging to navigate such a fast-changing landscape, this is a time of opportunity. It won't be easy. But if we work together, perhaps we can ensure that the multitude of platforms paves the way for ever-richer diversity, rather than survival of the blandest. ○

https://writersguild.org.uk
https://www.bbc.co.uk/writersroom/

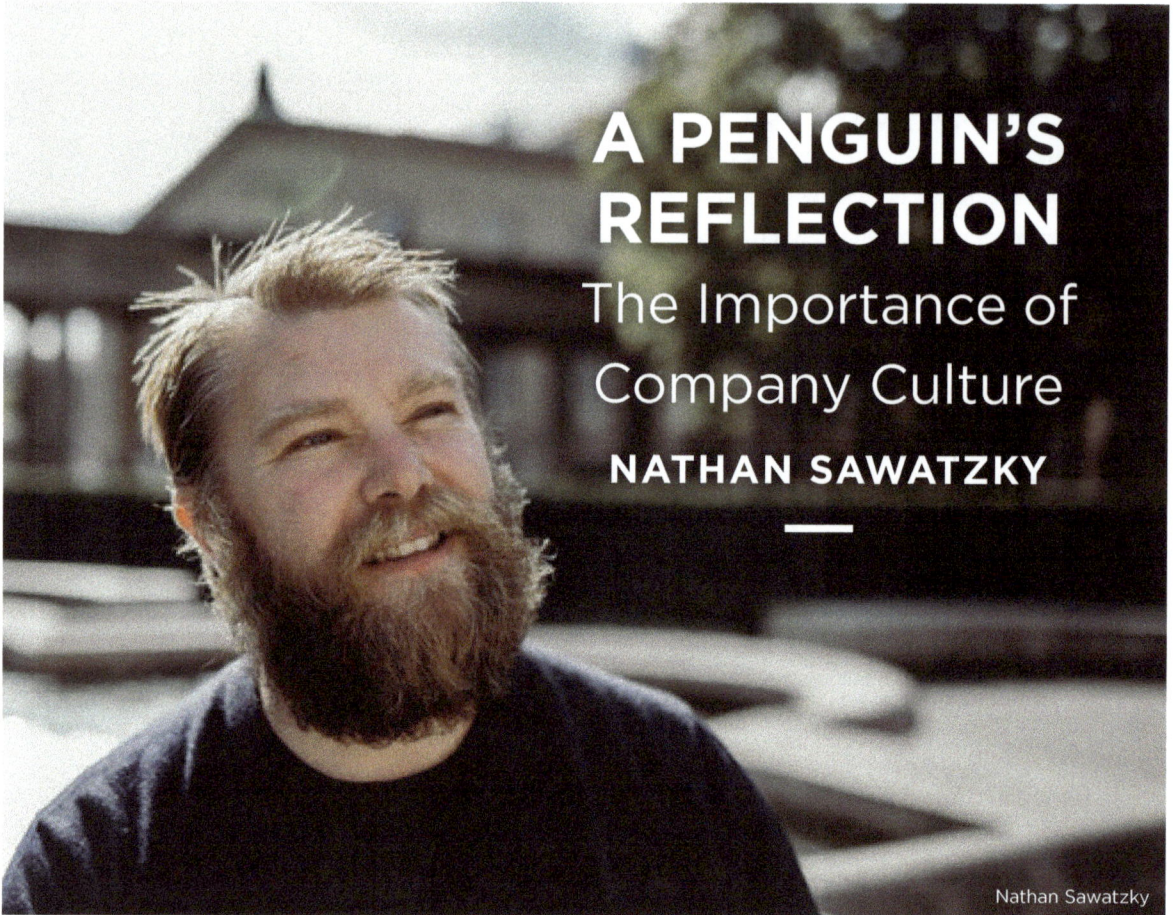

A PENGUIN'S REFLECTION
The Importance of Company Culture

NATHAN SAWATZKY

Nathan Sawatzky

Nearly fifteen years ago, I had the distinct privilege to join a soon-to-launch product called *Club Penguin*: a virtual world where children became penguins. My job was to manage the support channels and make sure the penguins behaved themselves; during my interview, the founders wanted to ensure I was up for building and leading a team … if ever the product grew big enough to need more than just myself, managing the community.

In short, it grew.

Seven years after the launch of *Club Penguin*, its purchase by The Walt Disney Company and the growth of that community support team to well over 200 people, operating out of six countries, I left with an overwhelming sense of gratitude. We were able to spend so many of those years holding strong to a culture which would, I believe, have honoured the community of children and their families that viewed *Club Penguin* as their personal online sandbox.

Our motto was:

"If it doesn't matter to an eight year old, it doesn't matter to us" – and while that may be oversimplifying what it means to establish a company culture that honours its audience, I can't overstate how often this little motto influenced big decisions about the way we operated.

Here's an example. In our headquarters in Kelowna, Canada, we had a large team of community support reps who managed the support and moderation of the community. While we had some folks that were over thirty, most of the crew was in their early twenties. Their ages didn't matter – except for the fact that most twenty-somethings don't *exclusively* listen to music without profanity.

But, collectively, the group agreed that we wouldn't want an eight year old to walk into any of our offices and hear music playing that contained lyrics they wouldn't be allowed to listen to. (Times have changed … but that's a different topic altogether!) If you popped on any of the support reps' headphones, you'd have heard them listening to music they felt would be appropriate for the community of players which they were actively supporting. Whatever these fine people listened to at home was of no impact; when they were at work, they were there for the community, including in ways that the community would never directly know about.

This is what it means to have integrity within the culture you're building for an audience.

Too often, I've walked into a studio where games are designed for children, but the culture seems entirely focused on trying to win the hiring war… "If you come work for us, you'll have everything you want – and we'll make it feel like you're at home in your basement." Not that creating a great environment isn't important – quite the opposite, actually – but there's a race to the lowest common denominator in company culture, especially within tech.

Can you imagine a company like Starbucks ever growing to the size it has reached, without a culture where people actually cared about coffee and the third-space? Or a company like Apple becoming so dominant, while having ugly offices and a lazy design approach?

Perks are great and we need to find ways to attract top talent to our companies. But we also need to establish cultures which foster our best and most compelling work

About a year into *Club Penguin*'s existence, we had two teams caring for the community: the day team and the night team. The day team had the enviable opportunity to work during the daylight hours; they frequently got to interact with the product team and just generally felt more connected. The night team were tight, but felt disconnected from the rest of the company.

We put the challenge out to the teams, to help us find a way to improve this.

One day, some of the people on the day team approached their team leader, asking for a small budget and some time to do something really cool for the night team. The team leader readily approved it and the day team set about doing a bunch of baking – the night team arrived later that day to a smorgasbord. The night team was moved by the gesture and the following week they stayed extra late to construct a giant pirate ship out of cardboard boxes for the morning team.

This went on and on over the course of the following year, with each team trying to outdo the other with creativity and kindness. Of course a team like this would be part of building *Club Penguin*'s reputation for being a strong and safe community for the millions of children who played there.

By way of example, that same year *Club Penguin* launched a programme called *Coins for Change*. Children would donate their virtual coins to one of three areas to promote change: children's health, the environment or children in developing countries. Coins were super valuable to the community; they were what children used to purchase items for their igloos or clothing for their penguins. They had to "work" hard for those coins.

But, during *Coins for Change*, the donations poured in. Children were more than willing to find little ways to help children around the world. In turn, the company gave real money to organisations focused on these areas and let the community know how they had made a difference.

We in the children's media industry have a responsibility to create content that betters the world for children. If the only way we do that is by focusing only on content, we may be missing out on the biggest opportunities. Strong, healthy, audience-focused company cultures create amazing environments, and attract the sort of people who not only ensures the full integrity of a product, but work towards creating a healthy future for our children – as they too grow up to be artists, developers and storytellers.

Give some thought to it by answering the following questions:

- If my target audience wandered into my studio, would they get the same message from walking the halls and witnessing interactions between team-members as they would from engaging in my product?

- Am I allowing my team to flourish by helping bridge the gap between our audience and the team?

- What's one change I could make that would get my audience excited to know about what's happening in my studio?

I'd love to hear from you, and learn about what you're doing to develop a culture which helps your team achieve amazing things. Send me a message at hello@nathansawatzky.com ◯

DEATH TO TV
Has the mini screen killed the small screen?

HANNAH SMITH

—

Rank the following from most to least watched – and, to the nearest million, estimate how many viewers each has had:

A. *I'm A Celebrity Get Me Out Of Here* (highest rated episode of 2018) – ITV – Nov/Dec 2018

B. A 20 second video of Stormi Jenner's feet – @KylieJenner – Instagram feed – Jan 2019

C. *Responding to Jake and Logan Paul* – KSI – YouTube – Feb 2018

Hannah Smith

There's no denying it – the ~~terrifying~~ wonderful world of online has fast become an intricate part of our culture … our lives! Do I scroll Instagram for 15 minutes before I've even brushed my teeth? Yes! Do I watch a YouTuber on my morning commute? Of course! Do I ever watch live TV? *Hellll* no … but I do binge a *lotttaaaa* Netflix. I'm a millennial – what you gonna do?

We find ourselves in a time when kids are not only consuming content online, but creating it. The internet is the best new platform for presenting talent. Where before, we saw the stars of children's TV rise through the ranks to become the faces of the biggest entertainment shows, we now have a brand-new space to discover the next big thing – and that's exciting!
No longer is the industry just for lucky drama school kids; the advent of vlogging

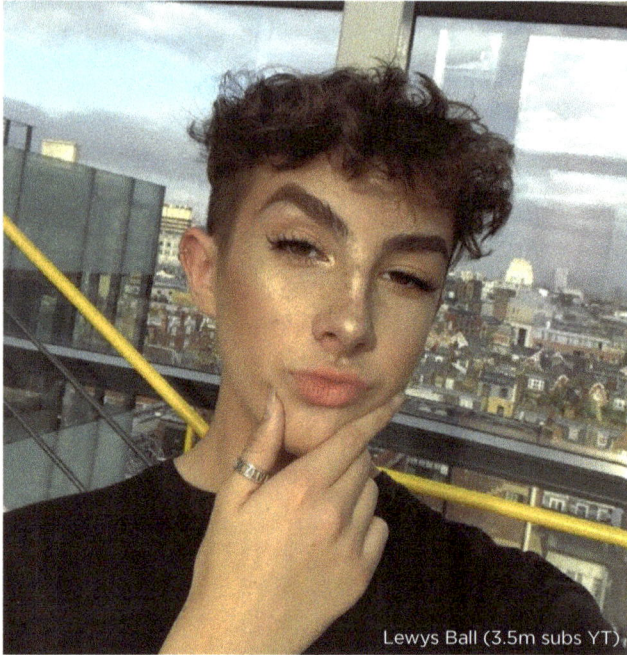

Lewys Ball (3.5m subs YT)

In 2017, our CBBC music show *The Playlist* brought YouTubers Lewys Ball and Jack Maynard (2 million subscribers) on board as presenters; in a single episode, the viewing figures rose by 150%.

Seeing viral faces on the linear channels is becoming more and more common. On CBBC alone we have Anna Maynard, Max and Harvey Mills, and Amelia Gething, to name but a few. They are superstars and their followers follow their every move … it's essentially free advertisement across multiple platforms! A great piece of talent with a decent following can surely only up your viewing figures – what's not to love?

If only everything was that easy. For

and online influencing has opened doors for everyone. All you need is a camera-phone (what a vintage term!) and you're off. Producers, directors and commissioners suddenly have access to the world's biggest showreel collection. Everyone wants to become an online star (my best friend even has a bot running his Instagram…) – and why wouldn't they? These influencers have the fame of 90's boybands and the opportunities to match.

They're called influencers for a reason. From merchandise to tours, Tik-Tok money gifts to huge ad-campaigns, these influencers are influencing a generation. And they can become a huge backing for your shows.

Jack Maynard (1.5m subs YT) // Max & Harvey (6m fans on TikTok)

Lewys Ball (3.5m subs YT) // Sabrina Carpenter (16.7m followers on Insta)

many vlogging superstars, this will be their first experience of being produced. It's always been just them – the talent, the producer, the director, the cam-op, the in-house post-department. So yes, bad habits may have been picked up. Live TV is a terrifying new world, and the rules and regulations that come with telly … well, that's unheard of. But anyone can learn and this is no reason to turn our backs on fresh new talent.

are making a LOT more than most of us are. British YouTube sensation DanTDM made $18.5 million in 2018 and American vlogger RyanToyReviews made $22 million. And he is only seven years old. SEVEN.)

It would be amiss to discuss the YouTube world without touching on those scandalous headlines. From faked kidnappings, racist comments, homophobic slurs and, of course, Logan Paul, it's no surprise that we can be a little sceptical

DanTDM (21m subs YT)

And of course, the nature of vlogging means that these content creators have become brands themselves. Channels and programmes no longer have full control of their talent, and that talent isn't just associated with one show. Their whole careers are showing their lives online and if their brand doesn't fully match your brand... Well, there's not a whole lot you can do about it – because I guarantee they

of the talent online. Without boundaries, these self-made superstars have had free reign on and offline. But we can't let the media tarnish our views of all online talent. Yes, a small handful of them should be steered clear of – but there is a huge pool of incredible (and safe!) talent to tap into.

So, with more and more of the younger generation switching off their TV sets and reaching for their devices, should we fear these online platforms? No! We need to stop separating these two worlds and start seeing everything for what it is – content and talent. Why make YouTube the enemy when we can work together? We need to put their fresh talent and ideas together with our years of broadcast experience, and create something amazing. ☺

Oh, and by the way…

B. **Instagram -** A 20 second video of Stormi Jenner's feet = **24 million** as of April 2019. (And for reference, as of April 2019, Kylie's baby announcement video was viewed over 182 million times across two platforms – Instagram and YouTube.)

C. **YouTube -** *Responding to Jake and Logan Paul* = **15 million** as of April 2019. (KSI's boxing fight with Logan Paul reached 21 million views in 24 hours.)

A. **ITV -** *I'm A Celebrity Get Me Out Of Here* = **14.17 million** (This is the highest rated episode of *I'm a Celebrity* ever)

KSI (20m subs YT, 4 billion views)

Operation Ouch game - Snot Apocalypse!

MEDIA MEDICINE

NIKKI STEARMAN

—

We have a great responsibility as media makers to teach our children about keeping fit and healthy. But what about children who aren't in perfect health? Content creators on every platform have so many exciting opportunities to improve medical experiences for all children.

In our house, my five year old son keeps our family's health in check. If the cereal box has a red label on the front, he'll tell you it's not healthy. I don't remember ever being this aware about my eating choices a few decades back, when pop tarts (with their icing topping and burning jam centres) were my go-to breakfast of choice.

Keeping fit and healthy is certainly a popular topic. It is high on the government agenda, with schemes like Change4Life encouraging families to eat well and exercise regularly. But there are great challenges for content creators who want to inform our children about their bodies and what they need to do to look after them. How do we do this without sounding too worthy, or repeating school lessons? And how can we keep these important

Get Well Soon Hospital

topics engaging, especially as children become older? Younger children want to know everything; so do older ones. The only difference is the older ones don't always want to ask.

CBeebies' *Get Well Soon* and CBBC's *Operation Ouch!* use charismatic medical professionals to engage children about how their bodies work. Both TV shows tailor their content to exactly the right level for their intended audiences and have won BAFTAs for their entertaining, accessible approach to delivering medical knowledge. *Get Well Soon* makes brilliant use of songs, with no topic out of bounds – as Dr Ranj's "Where Does Your Poo Come From?" song demonstrates. *Operation Ouch!* has a similar focus on the yuckier side of things, banking on children's innate curiosity about how their bodies work to experiment with extreme trials, often featuring the doctors themselves … as well as the odd gorilla!

Both shows have successful game extensions, using interactivity and play to delve deeper into health topics. *The Get Well Soon Hospital* game offers children the chance to explore the human body, and familiarise those who might be visiting a hospital for the first time not only with the environment, but also with some of the equipment and procedures they might encounter. Children can

X-ray a puppet patient to see what is inside – and it's not stuffing! As a mobile app, the game can be put to use directly within the hospital environment and doctors have been using it in hospital waiting rooms to help with children's anxieties.

Operation Ouch! translates the TV show's off-the-wall humour into hugely popular games on the CBBC website. *Snot Apocalypse!* requires players to run from an impending snot cloud and undertake challenging quick-fire mini games, like combing nits out of a patient's hair or getting a bed pan to a patient before he explodes. In the latest addition to the *Operation Ouch!* portfolio, *Invasion of the Snotulons*, players pass into Dr Chris's body and treat illness from the inside. It's a new iteration of the arcade classic; not a first person shooter, but a first person treater!

The interactivity these games offer gives children a chance to delve a bit deeper into health topics – to learn about their amazing bodies and about how they can be treated, if they need to be. But there is always more we can do. What other opportunities are there, for teaching children about staying well? It's helpful to look outside the media industry; for example, at the pioneering work of universities and hospitals to engage children.

Run by student doctors, Sheffield's Teddy Bear

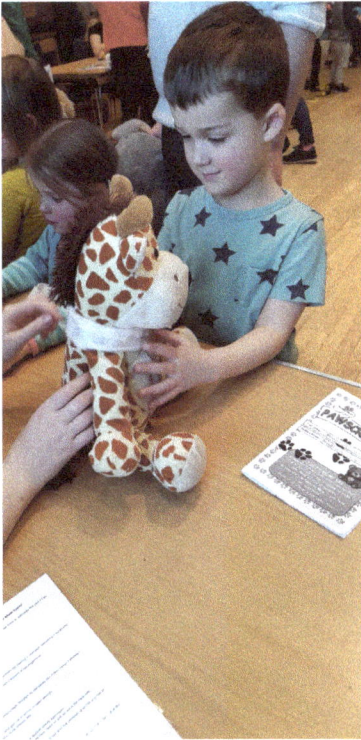

Sheffield's Teddy Bear Hospital

Hospital holds regular events for younger children to learn about their health. Each child can bring their teddy for a full health check: there are a variety of health stations where children can measure, weigh, bandage and X-ray their teddies, brush their teddies' teeth and even learn how to safely carry them across a road. It's engaging and it's fun – and focusing on a well-loved toy enables any potential worries or concerns to be projected elsewhere, and discussed openly. Poor Teddy has a sore tummy … how can we help him?

What about children who do have to visit the doctor or go into hospital – how can we, as content creators, support their experience of medical care?

Sometimes, taking well-loved content (a safe, known thing) into an unfamiliar environment can help to comfort and calm a child. When my son was having his preschool vaccinations, the first thing the nurse asked wasn't what I expected. She said, "What's your favourite thing to watch?" In 30 seconds she had Googled *Thomas & Friends* on YouTube; my son barely noticed the injection, as the theme tune played.

How else might we reassure apprehensive children? How can we be innovative in our delivery and content in these medical spaces? The potential for using Virtual Reality technology to help children during their time in hospital is hugely exciting. This may be as a pain distraction or to help them prepare for something unknown like a scan. Children need to lie still for 40 minutes to an hour in an MRI scan, which can be extremely loud during scanning sequences. As a result, both children and their parents are often anxious about their ability to cope.

Together with academic partners and the Sheffield Children's Hospital NHS Trust, Dr Dylan Yamada-Rice, Senior Researcher at Dubit, is creating a VR play kit for four to ten year olds, to help them prepare for the scan. The application of this relatively new technology offers huge potential for our future medical spaces.

What's next? Keep talking about health. Offer children (and their families) real opportunities to engage and learn about their bodies, and the wonders of medicine. Use our content to reassure those who are unwell, and to support them in medical spaces. Help inspire the next generation of healthcare professionals. But most of all: more media medicine, please … it's just what the doctor ordered! 🥚

HEARING VOICES
The art of voice acting
ALISON STEWART

—

The strand of sessions entitled "The Art of..." has become increasingly popular at the Children's Media Conference (CMC). The hour-long sessions are composed of two separate mini-masterclasses, given by experts in their particular field. Some of them focus on a specific Production-related skill (e.g. "The Art of the Theme Tune") and others deal with more cognitive topics (e.g. "The Art of Laughter"), but the aim of these sessions is always to offer insight, practical information and takeaway tips for anyone working in the business of children's media.

At CMC 2019, one of the showcased skills is "The Art of Voice Acting". The session is hosted by Marc Silk, one of the busiest voice artists in the UK, who works internationally across a range of media – animation, film, television, audio books, video games and commercial voice-over. He performs the voices of Johnny Bravo, Scooby Doo and Shaggy, characters for *Thunderbirds Are Go* and *LEGO*, Grandmaster Glitch from *Go Jetters*, and many, many more.

The documented history of "voice-over" begins in 1906, when a Canadian inventor called Reginald Fessenden successfully made the first wireless radio-broadcast to ships at sea – he voiced an entire programme which included music, Bible texts and Christmas messages.

The first voice-over for an animated character is credited to none other than Walt Disney, who created the voice for

Reginald Fessenden

Mickey Mouse in 1928 in his first animated short *Steamboat Willie*.

A giant name in the world of voice artistry is Mel Blanc, "the man of a thousand voices", who is widely recognized as the voice of virtually every major character in the classic Warner Brothers cartoons, including Bugs Bunny, Daffy Duck, Porky Pig, both Tweety Pie and Sylvester, and Yosemite Sam.

Don LaFontaine is the owner of another iconic voice. His speciality was movie trailers and his ominous, melodramatic baritone became known in the business as the "VOG", or "Voice of God". In his career he lent his voice to over 5,000 movie trailers and 350,000 commercials!

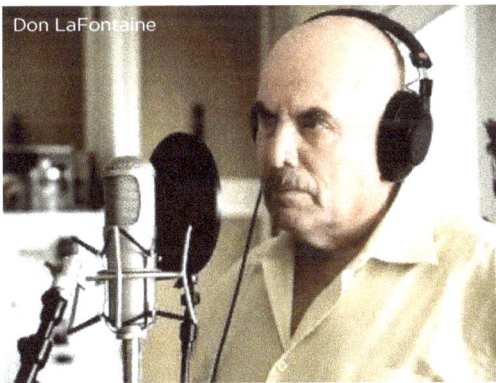
Don LaFontaine

In recent years, countless celebrities have offered their vocal talents to animated films and TV series – but the most famous voices in the animation world are often those of people whose names are largely unknown. Do you think you know your voice actors? Here's a challenge then … below is a list of artists who have been the original voices for some world-famous animated characters.

How many names can you match to their characters? (Answers below.)

Lisa Snowden-Fine

Don Messick

Bea Benaderet

Sterling Holloway

William Costelloe

Tress MacNeille

A voice for an animated character is not created by the voice artist alone. As each layer of a production takes shape, the ideas from the series-creator, producer, writer, director, visual and sound designers, composer and animators can all contribute to the way a character voice evolves. Conversely, the talent of the voice artist informs the ongoing work of the other creatives on the team. Thus, a character becomes fully-formed as all these contributors continue learning from each other.

So what is the art of a voice actor? Vital qualities (apart from a good voice!) are versatility, adaptability, agility of mind and the ability to infuse a character with individuality, authenticity and, in the case of most characters created for children, humour and warmth. When all this comes together, the audience becomes acquainted with a voice that will remain with them for a lifetime. ◌

Lisa Snowden-Fine - *original Peppa Pig (Season 1 only)*

Don Messick - *original Scooby Doo*

Bea Benaderet - *original Granny in Warner Brothers' Tweety Pie cartoons*

Sterling Holloway - *original Winnie the Pooh for Disney*

William Costelloe - *original Popeye*

Tress MacNeille - *Trick question! Tress has many hundreds of voice actor credits; my personal favourite is Crazy Cat Lady in The Simpsons.*

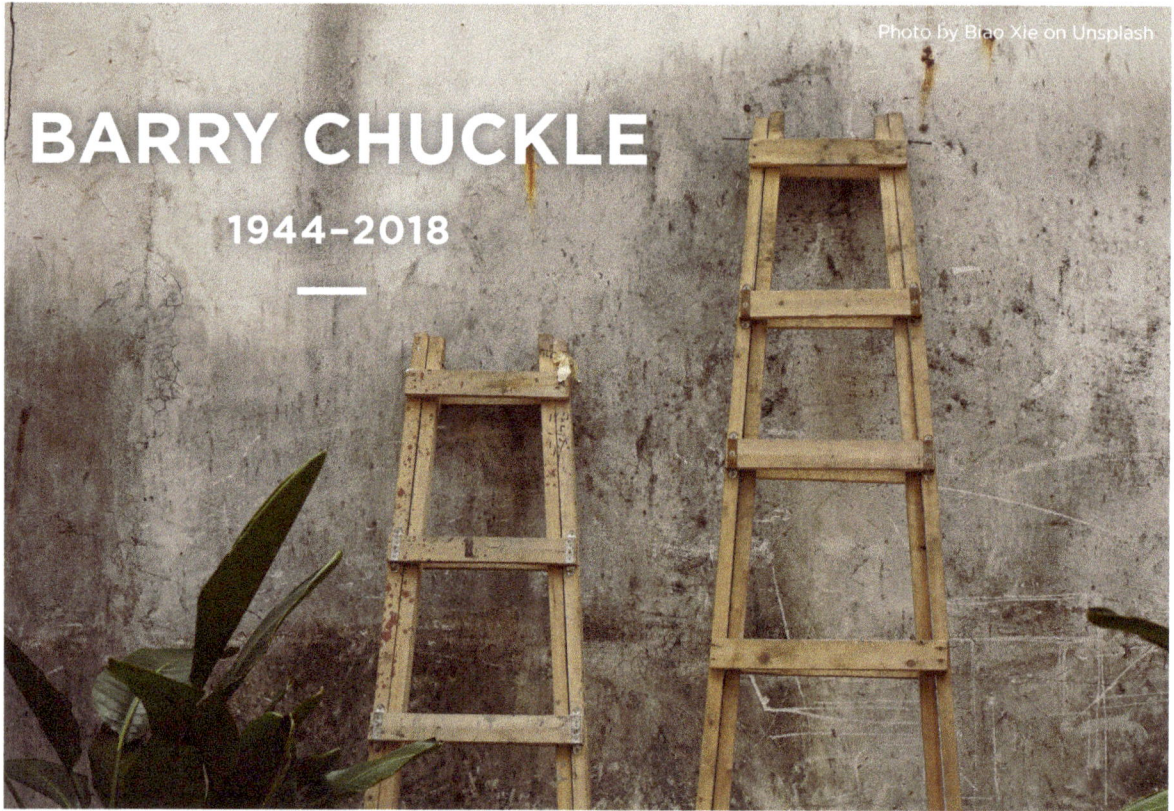

Photo by Biao Xie on Unsplash

BARRY CHUCKLE

1944–2018

The Chuckle Brothers won ITV's *Opportunity Knocks* in 1967 and *New Faces* in 1974. But it was a further 11 years before the BBC's *Chuckle Hounds* made Barry and Paul household names. Next, their classic BAFTA-nominated *ChuckleVision* ran for 21 series from 1987 to 2009 – a total of 292 episodes.

Prolific stage performers, Barry and Paul also appeared in 50 pantomimes: from the Robbers in *Babes in the Wood* (Malvern, 1967) to the Wicked Queen's bumbling Henchmen in *Snow White and the Seven Dwarfs* (Southampton, 2017).

Their final TV series together was *Chuckle Time* for Channel 5 in 2018.

When Barry died last August, aged 73, tributes poured in from fans on social media:

"Barry was one of life's rare gifts."

"Barry was an absolute diamond in the comedy industry!"

"Phenomenal talent, particularly with ladders."

"One of the hardest working and nicest guys in show business"

"Farewell to one half of Rotherham's finest brothers."

"Paul Chuckle: 'To me...'
The entire British nation: 'TO YOU...'".

By kind permission of the Yorkshire Post

JOHN CUNLIFFE

1933–2018

—

John Cunliffe lived in Ilkley for many years and was an important contributor to the town's literature festival.

An obituary in the *Ilkley Gazette* reads: "Left his Ilkley home in a deluge of rain on Thursday, September 20, 2018, never to return. Even the skies wept for John, the gifted creator of *Postman Pat*, *Rosie and Jim* and author of many earlier published collections of poetry and picture story books for children. John's last poetry collection, significantly entitled *Dare You Go*, has now come to fruition – for John has dared to go and he has gone."

Speaking to the *Westmorland Gazette* in 2009, Mr Cunliffe said the appeal of *Postman Pat* lay in the excitement children felt when the post arrived. "The postman to a child is someone who brings birthday cards and birthday presents – they are not aware that he also brings tax returns and bills!" ◷

(Reprinted by kind permission of the *Ilkley Gazette*.)

PETER FIRMIN

1928-2018

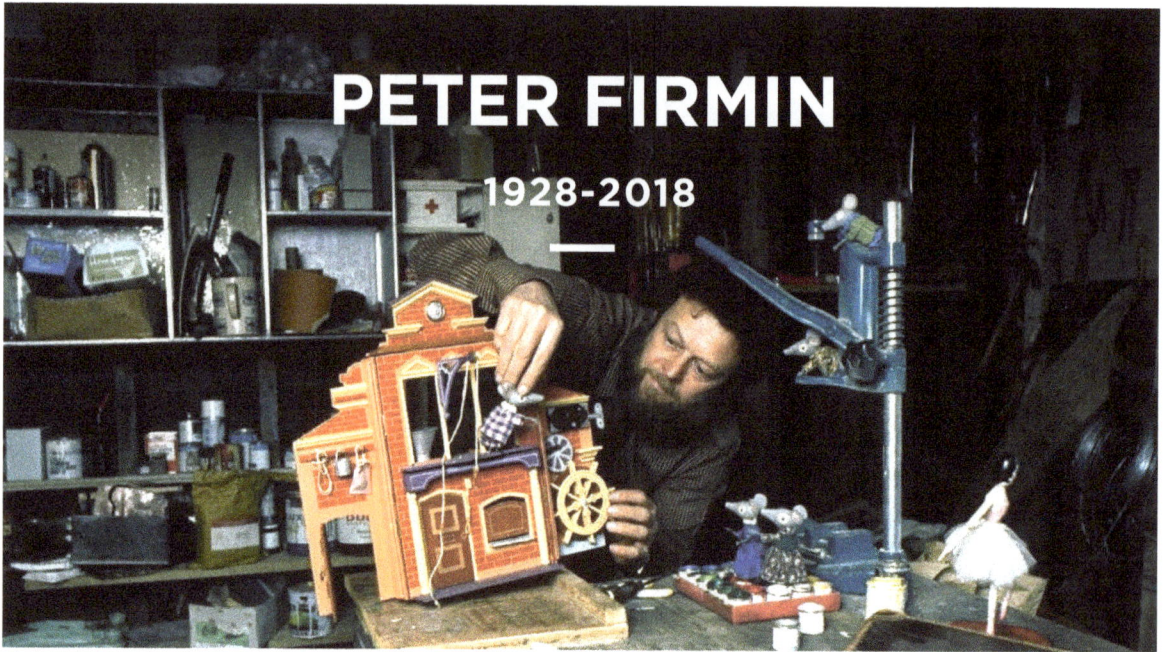

Peter Arthur Firmin was born in Harwich, Essex, in 1928. He attended the Central School of Art and Design in London – and later, while teaching at the Central School, he was approached by Oliver Postgate. Oliver was looking for "someone willing to do lots of drawing for very little money"

After being commissioned to make various TV projects, they tucked themselves away in the Kent countryside and created a series of TV worlds for children which remain popular to this day: those of *Noggin the Nog*, *Pogles' Wood*, *Ivor the Engine*, *the Clangers* and *Bagpuss*. Peter also devised and made the hugely popular cheeky fox Basil Brush.

Oliver was performer, animator and writer and Peter was illustrator and scene-and-puppet-maker. Their partnership lasted from 1958–86. *Bagpuss* was voted the most popular BBC children's show in 1999 and Peter received a Lifetime Achievement Award from BAFTA in 2014. In 2015, I had the great fortune to work with Peter on a new version of *The Clangers*.

As well as his TV and book work, Peter was a fine artist, creating many engravings, woodcuts and linocuts for all sorts of projects and charities.

Peter died on 1 July, 2018, leaving behind his wife, Joan, six daughters, and many grandchildren and great grandchildren.

A life well lived.

Daniel Postgate

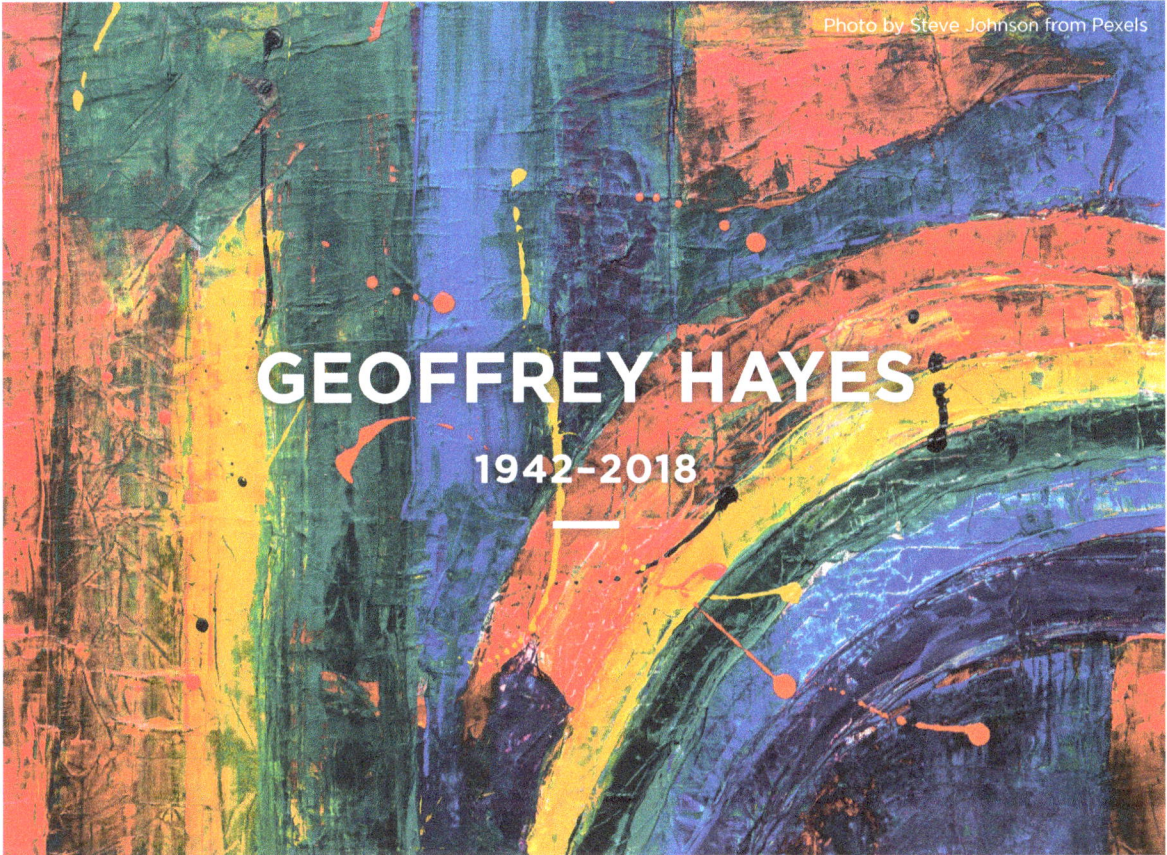
Photo by Steve Johnson from Pexels

GEOFFREY HAYES

1942–2018

In 2002, Geoffrey said the secret to *Rainbow*'s popularity was that it was full of "magic, innocence and imagination".

In 2015: "I'm very proud of *Rainbow*. People thank me for being an important part of their childhood – it's humbling."

And, speaking shortly after his 76th birthday last year: "We loved doing *Rainbow*; I certainly did. Twenty years of happiness, it really was."

In October 2018 tributes poured in from fans on social media:

"Genuinely heartbroken that Geoffrey Hayes has died. *Rainbow* was my religion."

"Geoffrey was a legend when I met him after a fantastic performance in Panto. He even drew me a picture of Zippy!"

"One of the nicest blokes I ever interviewed. Such a thrill to meet someone I'd watched growing up."

"Geoffrey – a pure legend in children's television. May you fly up above the streets and houses where the rainbow never ends."

Photo by Martin Martz from Pexels

JUDITH KERR OBE

1923-2019

Judith Kerr's publishing legacy is impressive; she was the author-illustrator of over 30 books, which sold millions of copies during her fifty-year career. *The Tiger Who Came to Tea* is a national favourite, as are the books in the *Mog* series.

It was her semi-autobiographical book, *When Hitler Stole Pink Rabbit*, which had a defining impact on how I personally related to books. This account of how she and her family were forced to flee Nazi Germany in the early thirties, told from her child's eye view, changed my life. It gripped me from start to finish, and I realised it was telling the story not just of Judith Kerr, but of countless other refugees – my German grandparents amongst them.

Reading became so much more than a pastime; she showed me that books change children's lives. Who wouldn't want to work in children's publishing, with literary giants like her to be inspired by?

Judith Kerr never forgot her good fortune in escaping the Nazi regime. "If you're blessed with a second chance at a life so many were deprived of, you can't waste it," she said – and she worked every day of her adult life.

Testament to that, her newest book, *The Curse of the School Rabbit*, was published in June 2019.

Julia Posen

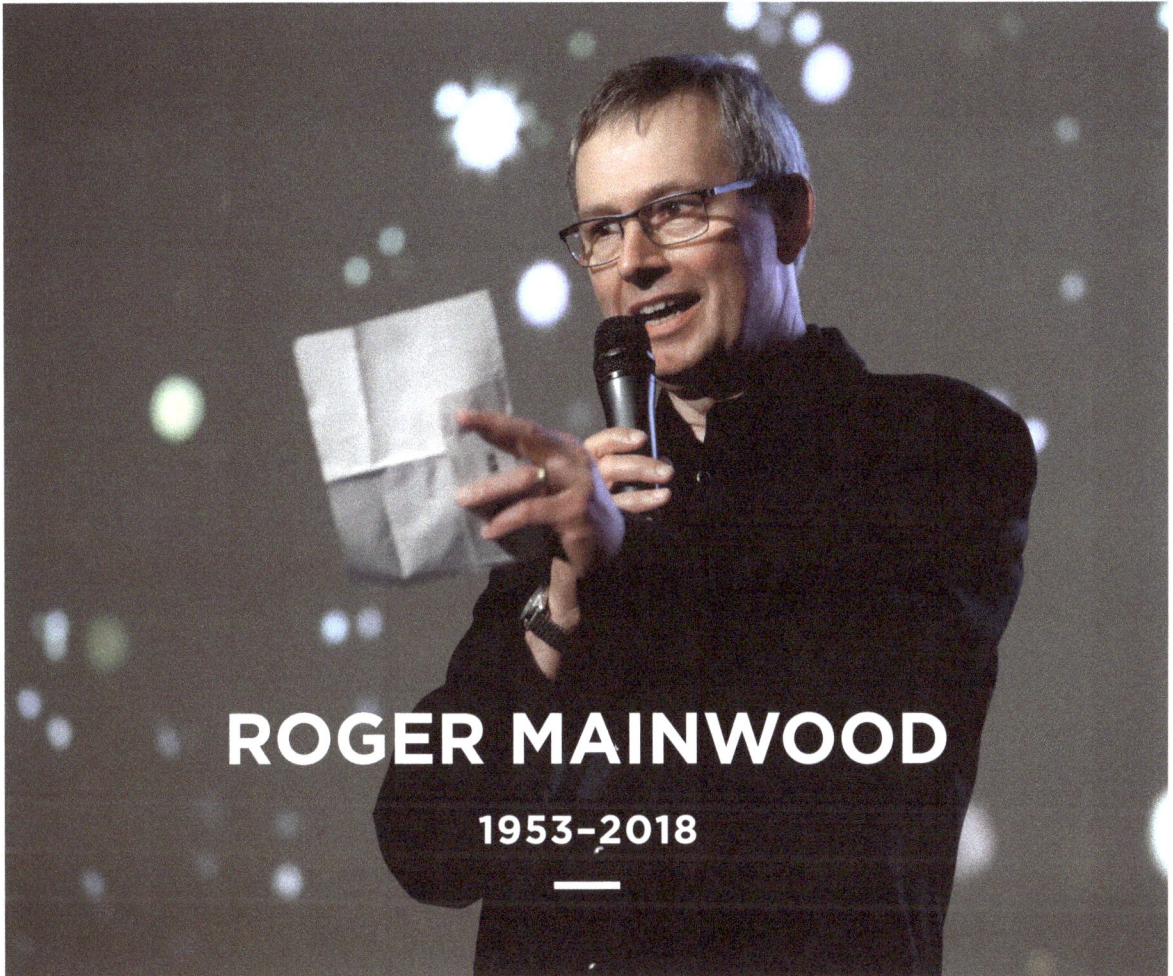

ROGER MAINWOOD

1953–2018

———

It was a real pleasure and a privilege to work with Roger on *Ethel & Ernest*, the animated film.

Roger was incredibly dedicated and famous for his 5 a.m. emails; he often stayed late in the studio to make sure everything was just right. Even Raymond Briggs, whose book the film was based on, was amazed by Roger's attention to detail – right down to researching the correct period light switches and linoleum patterns, and carefully calculating the exact height of a step from the hall to the kitchen in Raymond's childhood home.

Most of all, Roger was a very kind, thoughtful and principled person with a mischievous sense of humour, who was loved by all who worked with him.

His warmth and humanity are evident in every carefully crafted frame of *Ethel & Ernest*. ○

Camilla Deakin

Photo: BBC

MONICA SIMS OBE

1925 – 2018

—

When Monica Sims arrived in BBC Television Centre in 1967 the once thriving children's department was virtually defunct, consisting mainly of *Blue Peter,* and the newly arrived *Playschool.*

Monica rebuilt the department, laying the foundations of today's CBeebies and CBBC. She believed that children had as much right to a full service across all genres as adults did, a service which reflected their own interests and concerns. Persuading her BBC bosses that this was necessary, and needed the right funding was not easy. However Monica was both strong minded, and persuasive and gradually the new service emerged, including both period and contemporary drama, (including *Grange Hill*) and proper news in *Newsround*, plus a range of LE and factual series.

Monica was a great fighter, for the audience, for her staff, and for all women in the BBC. After leaving the children's department she became the first woman controller of Radio 4. ◗

Anna Home OBE

YOU DID IT!

CONTRIBUTORS

—

Dr Dea Birkett

Dr Dea Birkett founded and is Ringmaster of Circus250, the UK-wide celebration of 250 years of circus. An established broadcaster, Dea made *Who Killed the Circus?* for BBC World Service, an hour-long documentary on the end of Ringling Brothers circus, and *Circus Days*, *Circus Night*s, an hour-long documentary for Channel 4 on Dea's experiences as a circus artiste. Dea introduced and edited *Circus250* – the official brochure, documenting the history and current practice of circus. She is an award-winning writer and journalist, author of seven books including *Serpent in Paradise* and *Off the Beaten Track: Three Centuries of Women Travellers*. She contributes to the *Guardian*, *Mail on Sunday* and a wide range of publications, as well as regular commentating for the BBC and Irish media. Dea is Creative Director of ManyRiversFilms, a BAFTA-winning film company, making challenging dramas and documentaries. She is also Director of CultureKids Ireland, working with arts organisations so that they better include young people and children.

Candi Bloxham

Candi has over ten years experience as a digital producer, often working with emerging technologies for companies such as MTV and Fremantle Media. She has a MA in Character Animation and a MA in Digital Media, with a thesis on children's digital narrative. She has a breadth of experience managing and creating digital products and content for high profile TV shows, such as *MasterChef Australia*, *Australian Idol* and the MTV Music Awards. More recently, she worked as the VFX supervisor on *Strip the Cosmos* – a documentary series for the Discovery Channel.

Candi is now head octopus at Studio Octopi Kids, developing content with fun, diverse, colourful characters, which is both engaging and serves the purpose of making the world a better place.

Marc Ceccarelli

Marc Ceccarelli is the Co-Executive Producer on Nickelodeon's Emmy Award-winning *SpongeBob SquarePants* series, where he helps guide the creative trajectory of his comedic crew.

Ceccarelli graduated from CalArts in 1994, with a bachelor's degree in Live-Action Filmmaking. He then spent the next 15 years slogging away in the Halloween industry, designing and sculpting masks and props for Don Post Studios. He found his way into the animation industry through a back door that someone foolishly left open. Over the years, Ceccarelli has directed and produced various shorts for Nickelodeon, written episodes for two seasons of *Uncle Grandpa* and worked on cartoons for Disney, Film Roman and Adult Swim. Since 2010, Ceccarelli has worked in various capacities for *SpongeBob SquarePants*, including writing and storyboarding.

A fugitive from planet Bakersfield, Ceccarelli resides in Burbank, California, where much televisual cartoonification tends to happen.

Greg Childs

Greg Childs worked for over 25 years at the BBC, mainly as a director, producer and executive-producer of children's programmes. He created the first children's BBC websites and, as Head of Children's Digital, developed and launched the children's channels CBBC and CBeebies.

Greg left the BBC in 2004 and subsequently advised producers on digital, interactive and cross-platform strategies; and broadcasters on channel launches, digital futures and management support.

He was in the launch teams for Teachers TV and the CITV Channel in the UK, and was advisor to the Al Jazeera Children's Channel for three years, followed by a further three years consulting with the European Broadcasting Union on their Children's and Youth strategy.

Greg has been Editorial Director of the Children's Media Conference for the last fifteen years. He is also one of the Heads of Studies at the German Akademie Für Kindermedien, and is Director of the audience advocacy body – The Children's Media Foundation.

Alex Collier

Alex Collier has been a *Viz* comic co-editor and cartoonist for over twenty years. But that's not exactly "Children's Media", is it?

Alex also writes hilarious shows

for kids, including *Mr Bean*, *Danger Mouse*, *Dennis & Gnasher: Unleashed*, *Go Jetters* and *Class Dismissed*.

He is very handsome, has a full head of lustrous, flowing hair, doesn't have a double chin from certain angles, and appreciates being given the chance to write about himself in the third person.

Richard Cooper

Richard is Research Director at consultancy firm Ampere Analysis. He has more than 16 years' experience covering the Film and TV content markets, and advising firms on the development of their media businesses. Richard's clients include Hollywood studios, broadcasters, pay TV operators, regulators, video-on-demand services and investment firms. He regularly represents Ampere in TV and radio interviews, as well as at UK and international content-related conferences. He is also often quoted in national, international and trade press.

Tom Cousins

Tom Cousins is a Series Producer for BBC Children's, working across live action and animation. Tom has worked in development and production across CBeebies and CBBC programmes, most recently on the mixed-media series *Kit & Pup*.

Tom started out volunteering at the CMC ten years ago – back when the

Pizza Express Dinner was a couple of tables.

Nicky Cox MBE

Former BBC Children's Editorial Director, Nicky Cox is Founder and Editor-in-Chief of *First News*, the UK's only newspaper for children with more than two million readers. Nearly half of UK schools subscribe to *First News*.

Nicky also oversees the paper's online *First News Live!*, including a daily children's news bulletin made with Sky News.

She is Chief Executive of Fresh Start Media, an indie production company specialising in making factual content for, and about, children, including Sky TV children's news show *FYI*.

Nicky was made an MBE by the Queen for services to children and was given a Patron's award from the NSPCC for dedication to children. In 2014 Nicky was a Woman of Achievement in the Women of the Year Awards.

She is a Special Advisor to UNICEF, patron of the British Youth Citizen Awards, Ambassador of the Global Teacher Prize and a trustee of the British Blue Plaque Trust.

A mum of four, Nicky says children are 27% of the world's people but 100% of the future.

Camilla Deakin

Camilla Deakin is an award-winning Creative Producer, with a career spanning more than 25 years in the Film and TV industry.

After producing and directing a number of documentaries and arts programmes, Camilla joined the Arts and Music department of public service broadcaster Channel 4, where she soon rose to become Editor, Arts & Animation.

In 2002 Camilla set up Lupus Films with her friend and colleague Ruth Fielding, and the company has grown to become one of the UK's leading animation studios, with an international reputation for beautifully crafted film adaptations of classic children's literature.

Recent productions include a hand-drawn animated feature film adaptation of Raymond Brigg's graphic novel *Ethel & Ernest* and a half-hour special based on Michael Rosen and Helen Oxenbury's much-loved children's book *We're Going on a Bear Hunt*.

Lupus Films is currently in production with an animated adaptation of Judith Kerr's best-selling book *The Tiger Who Came to Tea*.

Sarah De Caux

Sarah De Caux is a Senior Research Director in Spirit, Join the Dots' in-house team of qualitative practitioners.

She has worked in research since 2002, and remains curious about people. Over the years, Sarah has researched most areas – but, in particular, she has a deep understanding of digital and its role in people's lives. Prior to joining the Dots, she worked at a research agency where she was based in both the UK and China.

Sarah is a member of the Association for Qualitative Research, MRS, ESOMAR and holds a CIM Professional Diploma.

In 2018 she was a finalist (along with the client team at Auto Trader) for the AQR Prosper Riley Smith Award for Qualitative Excellence.

Stuart Dredge

Stuart Dredge is a freelance journalist covering digital media and children's technology. He writes articles for *Music Ally* and *The Week Junior* magazine, and reports on kids and tech for ContempoPlay.

Jackie Edwards

Jackie joined the BFI in 2019, to shape and launch the Young Audiences Content Fund. She was formerly the BBC's Head of Children's Acquisitions and Independent Animation, delivering programming for 0–16 year olds. As well as overseeing the strategy for her department, Edwards was responsible for pre-buying and acquiring live-action and animated programming.

Edwards first joined the BBC in 2008 as CBeebies Content Manager, and later became Executive Producer, working on programmes including *Tree Fu Tom*, *Octonauts*, *Bing*, *Rastamouse* and *The Clangers*.

She started her television career in animation in 1995 as a production assistant with Hibbert Ralph Entertainment (later Silver Fox Films), going on to produce many prestigious specials and award-winning series. Prior to the BBC, Edwards was a freelancer, working on the development, finance and production of shows for a variety of companies – such as LEGO, CBBC, Three Stones Media and Mackinnon and Saunders.

Fox Fisher

Fox Fisher (Honorary Doctorate and MA in Sequential Design & Illustration) is an award-winning artist, filmmaker and trans rights campaigner.

Fox co-founded Trans Pride Brighton, helped to set up the Trans Acting course at the Royal Central School of Speech and Drama (with Gendered Intelligence), runs the My Genderation film project, co-created the books *Trans Teen Survival Guide* and *Are You A Boy Or Are You A Girl*, and is an advisor for All About Trans, facilitating interactions with the mainstream media.

Fox just completed a documentary about being non-binary in the UK, titled *I AM THEY*.

Follow Fox on Instagram and Twitter, under the handle @thefoxfisher

Anna Home OBE

Anna began working for the BBC in 1960 and started working in the children's department in 1964. She has won many accolades, including a BAFTA lifetime achievement award. Anna was the first Chair of the BAFTA Children's Committee, and has chaired both the EBU Children's and Youth Working Group and the Prix Jeunesse International Advisory Board. She was also the Chair of the Save Kids' TV Campaign Executive Committee and the Showcomotion children's media conference.

She now Chairs the Board of the CMC (Children's Media Conference) and the Children's Media Foundation, and is a Board member of Screen South.

Vicky Ireland MBE FRSA

Vicky worked as an actor and teacher in the original Theatre-in-Education company at the Belgrade Theatre, Coventry. For twelve years, she was also the presenter of the BBC's children's programme *Words and Pictures*.

As Artistic Director of Polka Theatre, London, from 1988–2002, Vicky directed, produced and commissioned new theatre-writing for children; she adapted and directed six books by Jacqueline Wilson, the bestselling author and former Children's Laureate, for Polka and Watershed productions. Her television writing includes two series of adaptations of Allan Ahlberg's

Happy Families books for the BBC, which received a Writer's Guild of Great Britain nomination. Along with Paul Harman, Vicky also co-edited the book *50 Best Plays for Young Audiences*, published by Aurora Metro Press.

In 2002, Vicky was awarded the MBE medal in the Queen's Jubilee Birthday Honours list for services to children's drama – the first of its kind.

She is a Patron of Polka Theatre and the Chair of Action for Children's Arts.

Becky Jones

Becky is an Executive Producer at Boojum Media, an independent company specialising in education content and documentaries for children.

Becky was formerly Executive Producer for primary and secondary news and curriculum content at Discovery Education, before she was promoted to Head of News and Video.

Through her career, she has been a Producer/Director at the BBC, Granada, LWT, C4, C5 and A&E Networks on award-winning history, science and arts series, ranging from *Horizon* to *Child of our Time*. She was Head of Development at leading indie Wag TV.

Becky is also a journalist and the co-author of a series of non-fiction books for children: *Adventure Walks* and *The Bumper Book of London*. She is a Member of William Tyndale Primary School in London.

Becky founded Boojum Media in 2018.
Mobile: 07751 909980
Twitter: @beckyjonescm

Tessa Moore

Tessa Moore is a family entertainment expert who has had a broad career in international brand development and marketing, working for global businesses including Virgin Publishing, Disney and FremantleMedia.

At FremantleMedia, Tessa was responsible for global preschool hits *Kate & Mim-Mim* and *Tree Fu Tom*, and the reboot of the family favourite *Danger Mouse*.

During her prior career at Disney, she developed European growth strategies for many of Disney's evergreen franchises, including Mickey Mouse and Winnie the Pooh.

Tessa is now a consultant, specialising in creating strategic growth plans and provides business development, IP monetisation advice and marketing support to the global industry.

Rachel Murrell

Rachel is a scriptwriter, journalist and the creator of "dress testing", a Bechdel Test for kids' content.

Her more than 180 writing credits include episodes of *PJ Masks*, *Ask Lara*, *Little Princess* and more – and her work has been nominated for a Children's BAFTA, a British Animation Award and an International Kids' Emmy.

Rachel was a finalist in the 2017 BAFTA/Rocliffe New Writing for Children Awards for her original circus drama *UpsideDown*.

She's loves contemporary circus and also juggles. Badly.

Alison Norrington

Alison is a best-selling novelist, playwright and journalist, and a PhD researcher with a Masters in Creative Writing and New Media. She is Conference Chair for StoryWorld Conference LA, Exec Producer of Virtual Reality sessions for CMC and a two-time TEDx speaker. She is also a BAFTA Guru and member of the International Academy of Television Arts and Sciences, The Writers Guild of Great Britain and Women in Film and TV. She is Founder and Chief Creative Director of storycentral (online at www. storycentral.com; @storycentral on Twitter), a London-based entertainment studio that incubates and develops ground-breaking transmedia properties with global partners in film, television, animation, publishing, advertising, branding, theme parks, Virtual Reality and gaming. As CEO/CCO of storycentral, Alison has worked on a range of intellectual properties that are founded on robust story worlds with strong core themes, and genuine and relevant touch-points across a host of media channels. She specialises in storytelling that amplifies fan incubation and engagement, experience design, extending IP and franchises, community build through story and storyworld strategy, incubation and development – all centered around a robust core of story architecture, theme, awareness of audience and experience design.

Julia Posen

Julia is a children's media freelancer, working on a range of publishing and TV properties.

Previously, Julia was responsible for building new business and global opportunities for the Group Rights and Development division at Walker Books. Julia joined Walker in 2010 as Marketing, Brand and Licensing Director.

This followed twelve years at the BBC, where she held a number of senior posts – including Children's Commercial Director at BBC Worldwide.

Daniel Postgate

Daniel Postgate is the son of the filmmaker Oliver Postgate. He started his career as a cartoonist and strip cartoonist for *The Sunday Times*, *The Radio Times* and *Loot*, and produced a syndicated "fact cartoon" – *Did You Know?*

Daniel has written and illustrated over fifty children's books, winning the Nottingham and Norfolk Children's book awards and becoming shortlisted for the Stockport and Sheffield Children's book awards. He is now a BAFTA-winning scriptwriter on the new version of *The Clangers*.

He lives with his family in Whitstable, Kent.

Belinda Ioni Rasmussen

Belinda Ioni Rasmussen heads up Macmillan Children's Books, a division of Pan Macmillan and home to *The Gruffalo*, among many other bestselling children's brands, authors and illustrators.

Belinda joined Pan Macmillan seven years ago and has led the business through six consecutive years of revenue and volume growth, driven by focus on brand management, IP extensions of key properties and successful investment in new areas of publishing, including ramping up Macmillan Children's licensed properties and strengthening the fiction side of the business.

Before Macmillan, Belinda was the MD of Carlton Publishing Group. During her time at the indie, she expanded the children's publishing programme and experimented with digitally enhanced eBooks and apps. Belinda also spent nine years at Egmont in a range of senior roles from Rights, Special Sales, International Sales and New Business Development to Director of Egmont Press (the then fiction and picture-book division of Egmont). During her time at Egmont, she took an MBA from the London Business School.

Emma Reeves

Emma's TV work includes three series of *Eve* (CBBC; lead-writer and co-creator), *The Worst Witch* (Series 1, lead-writer), *The Dumping Ground*, *Tracy Beaker Returns*, *Young Dracula*, *Hetty Feather* and *The Story of Tracy Beaker*. In 2016, she received the Writers' Guild Award for Best Children's TV Episode for *Eve*. Two of Emma's TV episodes (*The Dumping Ground* and *Hetty Feather*) were nominated for the 2016 Children's BAFTA for Best Drama. She also writes stage and audio drama.

Nate Sawatzky

Nate began his professional career building and leading the community support team at *Club Penguin*, a massively successful children's virtual world which was purchased by the Walt Disney Company in 2007. At Disney, Nate's role expanded to overseeing support and community policy for Disney Online Studios. Since leaving Disney, Nate has spent the past eight years working with small and large companies, such as Tiny Speck, kidSAFE and Facebook, to develop meaningful community policies and practices. He also continues to contribute to the broader conversations, both academically and within the private sector, around technology and the way society interacts with it.

Hannah Smith

Multiple RTS winner and BAFTA nominee Hannah Smith has been

dabbling in television since she was at school. Only a few years later, she moved from Edinburgh to London to join Strawberry Blond TV.

Since, Hannah has produced for Disney, UKTV, BBC 4 and is currently the Series Producer on CBBC's *The Playlist*.

When she's not up to her eyes in spreadsheets, Hannah can be found travelling the world in search of the best cheeses!

Nikki Stearman

Nikki is a Senior Game Designer at Dubit, creating playful and meaningful digital experiences for children. She is passionate about all things kids, from major children's entertainment brands to innovative projects for non-profit and government organisations.

Nikki's career in children's digital media stretches back 14 years. She started as a specialist in e-learning content before moving into games, where she won a BAFTA for her work at CBBC.

Alison Stewart

Alison has worked in children's media production for most of her career: twice at the BBC and also as a freelance Series Producer, Director, and Scriptwriter. Her most recent role at the BBC was Head of CBeebies Production. Alison left the BBC in 2018 and since then has been writing and consulting. She also

leads on a project called "Hope Works" (www.hopeworksproject.com), which she co-founded with Lucy Murphy, Head of Kids' Content at Sky. This global initiative launched on World Children's Day, 20 November, 2018, and discussions are taking place with broadcasters to produce a second series of films this year.

Juliet Tzabar

Juliet has worked in digital media for over 16 years. Following an early career in the art departments of television dramas, Juliet moved into digital media in 2000. She has since specialised in delivering interactive projects with a broadcast tie-in, and a focus on the children and families audience. Juliet joined Plug-in Media in 2007, and as CEO has overseen the company's growth and success, establishing it as one of the UK's leading digital production companies. She takes an Executive Producer role on many of the company's projects, including the BAFTA-winning interactive projects: *Big and Small*, *Zingzillas* and *Get Well Soon Hospital*. Since 2013, Juliet has been leading the company's original IP strategy, driving the "digital-first" success of *Tee and Mo*, from ten web games via short-form content to a 50×7' animated TV series. In 2011, Juliet was shortlisted for the Women in Technology Entrepreneur of the Year Award.

Camilla Umar

Cam is your Children's Media Yearbook 2019 designer! She divides her days between her design business – cutoutandkeep – and her tiny yoga empire, Loop Yoga.

As a designer she regularly works with Sheffield Theatres, Lawrence Bately Theatre Huddersfield, and the CMC and CMF, as well as small businesses and start-ups.

The rest of the time she can be found thinking about, talking about, teaching, or travelling between, her community yoga classes ... and generally having a lovely time..
www.cutoutandkeep.co.uk
www.loopyoga.co.uk

Vincent Waller

Vincent Waller is the Co-Executive Producer on Nickelodeon's Emmy Award-winning *SpongeBob SquarePants*, where he has been a veteran of the show for over 14 years. A writer, cartoonist and director, Waller worked his way up from doing caricatures on Bourbon Street to working on Marvel's *The Savage Tales* and *The Savage Sword of Conan*, where he eventually found his way to Animation.

In addition to writing and directing several episodes of Nickelodeon's *The Ren & Stimpy Show*, Waller also produced and directed shorts for Fred Seibert's *Oh Yeah! Cartoons*. He also co-created *What is Funny*?, adapted the Harvey Kurtzman comic *Hey Look!* and created *Pete Patrick Private Investigator*.

In 2000, Waller joined *SpongeBob SquarePants* as a writer, where he served in various capacities ranging from a storyboard artist, Director and Creative Director. He most recently served as Creative Director for Paramount's hit feature film *The SpongeBob Movie: Sponge Out of Water*.

Originally a resident of Texas, Waller currently resides deep in North Hollywood. In between absorbing as much entertainment as possible, Waller also enjoys drawing and hiking in his free time.

Heather Wardle

Funded by Wellcome, Heather is exploring youth gambling behaviour and its relationship with technological change.

She is Deputy Chair of the Advisory Board for Safer Gambling, an independent group which provides advice on policy and practice to the Gambling Commission.

Previously, she was a Research Director at NatCen Social Research, leading their programme of work on gambling – including the British Gambling Prevalence Survey.

Becky Watson

Becky Watson is a Senior Editor at Walker Books, the independent children's publisher – home to the classic picture-books *Guess How Much I Love You?* and *Where's Wally?*, #1 *New York Times* bestseller *The Hate U Give* and many more beautiful books besides.

Becky has worked on a little of everything at Walker, including narrative non-fiction, novels for children of all ages, picture-books and poetry anthologies. Along the way, she has had the excellent fortune to work with a number of supremely talented authors and illustrators.

This is Becky's first year text-editing the Children's Media Yearbook; she's loved reading about all these different aspects of children's media, from the Clangers to British circus!

Mark Wilson

Mark bluffed his way into Radio 3, claiming he could touch type. Decades later, he's editing this Yearbook – ever so grateful that keyboards are less messy than inky golf balls, smudgy carbon and sticky Tipp-Ex.

A cut 'n' paste of Mark's career includes writer, producer and director: BBC TV Promotions, the CBBC *Broom Cupboard* with Edd the Duck and GMTV worldwide travel guides; also Commissioning Editor for CITV Mornings and Head of Digital for *Kuu Kuu Harajuku* on Nick USA.

Freelancing as a creative producer, script and lyric writer, Mark's current projects include: *Booba* on Netflix, *A Cheesy Musical* (movie in development) and a global documentary series presented by lycra legend Mr. Motivator.

Current memberships: the Writers' Guild of Great Britain, CMC Advisory Committee, CMF Executive Group, and PRS for Music.

Mark is also a distinguished alumnus of the BBC Langham Typing School.

mistermarkwilson@gmail.com
https://uk.linkedin.com/in/mistermarkwilson

Will Young

Will Young has spent much of the last two decades at the forefront of pop in the UK, having won the inaugural series of *Pop Idol* at the age of just 22. One of the very first success stories of televised talent shows, Will Young's *Pop Idol* victory and unprecedented, chart-storming career became an iconic part of noughties pop culture.

Four #1 and two #2 chart-topping albums, two Brit Awards and four UK #1 singles followed, with such hits as "Leave Right Now" and "Jealousy". An acting career blossomed concurrently, including Baz Lurhmann's *Strictly Ballroom* in the West End, and presenting gigs on TV and radio.

Young is also an active and vocal campaigner for the LGBT movement, and his podcast *Homo Sapiens* – which he co-created and co-presents with filmmaker Chris Sweeney – has been such a huge success that Young and Sweeney are planning to grow it into a festival, and potentially expand into children's books with a focus on diversity.

The Children's Media
FOUNDATION

We need your support:

www.thechildrensmediafoundation.org

TAH-DAH!
Section headers take a bow
—

INTERJECTIONS
Schoolhouse Rock Live! (Ahrens)

ZERO TO HERO
Disney's *Hercules* (Menken/Zippel)

BACK TO SCHOOL AGAIN
Grease 2 (St. Louis/Greenfield)

THE ROSES OF SUCCESS
Chitty Chitty Bang Bang (Sherman/Sherman)

REVIEWING THE SITUATION
Oliver! (Bart)

OPTIMISTIC VOICES
The Wizard of Oz (Harburg/Harburg/Arlen/Stothart)

TELLY
Matilda the Musical (Minchin)

SO LONG, FAREWELL
The Sound of Music (Rogers/Hammerstein)

YOU DID IT!
My Fair Lady (Lerner/Loewe)

The Children's Media
FOUNDATION

www.ingramcontent.com/pod-product-compliance
Lightning Source LLC
Chambersburg PA
CBHW042350030426
42336CB00025B/3431